YORK NOTES

General Editors: Professor A.N. Jeffares (*University of Stirling*) & Professor Suheil Bushrui (*American University of Beirut*)

John Milton

PARADISE LOST
BOOKS I & II

Notes by Richard James Beck

OBE MA (OXFORD) PH D (ST ANDREWS)
Former Professor, University of Malta

LONGMAN
YORK PRESS

YORK PRESS
Immeuble Esseily, Place Riad Solh, Beirut.

LONGMAN GROUP LIMITED
London
Associated companies, branches and representatives
throughout the world

© Librairie du Liban 1980

First published 1980
ISBN 0 582 78218 X
Printed in Hong Kong by
Sing Cheong Printing Co Ltd

Contents

Part 1: Introduction   *page* 5
   Milton's times   5
   Milton's life   6
   Milton's cosmology   10
   The epic   11
   A note on the text   14

Part 2: Summaries   15
   A general summary   15
   Detailed summaries   16

Part 3: Commentary   49
   Cosmology   49
   Theology   50
   Epic and the epic hero   52
   Style   59

Part 4: Hints for study   62
   Answering questions on the text   62
   Type of question set on *Paradise Lost*, Books I and II   64
   Specimen question   64

Part 5: Suggestions for further reading   67

The author of these notes   69

Part 1

Introduction

Milton's times

The world into which John Milton was born in 1608 was a troubled and confused one; and, until his death in 1674, Milton lived through a period of turmoil and violent change. By 1608 the King, James I, had been on the throne of England for five years; coming south from Scotland after the death of Elizabeth I, he lacked the popularity of his doughty predecessor, on both national and personal grounds. Also, he was extravagant in an age when the royal revenues were steadily decreasing in value and, believing that he had been called to rule by God's command rather than by the will of the people or the consent of their representatives, James clashed frequently and violently with Parliament over the control of the country's government, and particularly its finances. An early struggle for control of the judges was resolved, by 1621, in favour of Parliament. King James also thought that he should control the Church through its bishops; but a group of men, increasing in numbers and strength as the years went by, believed that the English Reformation, begun by Henry VIII with the double purpose of divorcing a queen who could not give him a male heir and of stripping the many rich monasteries and abbeys of their treasures, scarcely justified its name. Realising that such abuses as one priest holding more than one living were being retained, and that the authority of the Pope had been replaced by that of the King as head of the English Church, these men, the Puritans, strove for a more austere and purer form of worship and Church organisation. Puritanism is not a religion, nor confined to any one sect: it is an attitude of mind. These two forces of Puritanism and Parliamentarianism together resisted royal absolutism, at first by constitutional means, seeking to make the granting of revenue dependent upon the reform of abuses; and, from 1642 onwards, by force of arms.

James I's son and successor, Charles I, quarrelled bitterly with his Parliaments from his accession in 1625 until 1629, when he determined to rule without a parliament at all; this period was called the Personal Rule. Forced by a Scottish invasion to recall Parliament in 1640 to vote funds for an army, Charles disagreed with them all over again, saw his chief minister, Strafford, and his Archbishop of Canterbury, Laud, removed from authority and executed, and, finally, in 1642, took up arms to crush the forces of Parliament. Successful in the early stages of the war, Charles faced a powerful combination in the alliance of Parliament with the Scottish Covenanters, the loyalty of London to the Parliamentary cause, and the brilliant generalship of Oliver Cromwell. Charles's fortunes declined, he was beaten in decisive battles at Marston Moor in 1644 and Naseby in 1645, surrendered, was imprisoned, tried, condemned and beheaded in 1649. Thereafter Cromwell ruled England as Lord Protector until his death in 1658; but the Commonwealth had become increasingly unpopular, and there was no strong character to succeed Cromwell. So in 1660 the royal house of Stuart was restored to the English throne in the person of Charles II, morally profligate but politically astute. He had been on the throne for fourteen years when Milton died in 1674, and a further fourteen years were to pass before a second revolution continued the process of securing Parliamentary rule in England and making its monarchy more constitutional.

Milton's life

No other English poet has been so closely involved in the events of his time as Milton; and only Wordsworth has ever told us so much about himself. In Milton's case there were two reasons for this: much of his work as Latin Secretary to Cromwell consisted of writing pamphlets justifying government policy, and these pamphlets and the ones inspired by the exiled Royalists did not hesitate to stoop to the most scurrilous personal details—and Milton sought to counter any such attacks on him by producing autobiographical evidence. The second reason is that he felt from an early age that he was destined 'to leave something so written to after-times as they should not willingly let it die', and therefore believed that posterity would wish to know as much as possible about him. In his pamphlet *The Second Defence of the People of England*, which is in large part a defence of himself in answer to a detractor, Milton tells us:

> My father destined me from a child to the pursuits of literature; and my appetite for knowledge was so voracious, that, from twelve years of age, I hardly ever left my studies, or went to bed before midnight. This primarily led to my loss of sight. My eyes were naturally weak, and I was subject to frequent head-aches; which, however, could not chill the ardour of my curiosity, or retard the progress of my improvement. My father had me daily instructed in the grammar-school, and by other masters at home. He then, after I had acquired a proficiency in various languages, and had made a considerable progress in philosophy, sent me to the University of Cambridge. Here I passed seven years in the usual course of instruction and study, with

the approbation of the good, and without any stain upon my character, till I took the degree of Master of Arts. After this I did not, as this miscreant feigns, run away into Italy, but of my own accord retired to my father's house, whither I was accompanied by the regrets of most of the fellows of the college, who shewed me no common marks of friendship and esteem. On my father's estate, where he had determined to pass the remainder of his days, I enjoyed an interval of uninterrupted leisure, which I entirely devoted to the perusal of the Greek and Latin classics; though I occasionally visited the metropolis, either for the sake of purchasing books, or of learning something new in mathematics or in music, in which I, at that time, found a source of pleasure and amusement. In this manner I spent five years till my mother's death.*

There is much of interest in this passage: the reference to Milton's weak eyes—the poet who wrote *Paradise Lost* was at the time of writing it totally blind, claiming that he had sacrificed his eyes in the service of liberty and Cromwell's government; his affection for and gratitude to his father, which reveals a gentler side of an otherwise unloving nature (his only real friend, Charles Diodati, died young, and the famous elegy on Lycidas was in fact a poem more concerned with Milton than with his Cambridge contemporary Edward King); and the years of dedication to private study, financed by his father, which resulted in *Paradise Lost*'s being a poem difficult for the modern reader to understand by reason of its extensive learning and wealth of allusion.

After Cambridge and Horton (the estate in Buckinghamshire referred to in the quotation), Milton began a European tour. He visited Galileo in Fiesole, near Florence; Galileo is the only one of Milton's contemporaries to merit a mention in *Paradise Lost* (he is named in V.260 and is the 'Tuscan artist' of I.288). Milton cut short his tour because of the situation in England, but did not hurry unduly on his way home, and did not join the armies of the Parliament on his return, devoting himself instead to the education of his two nephews, the Phillips brothers. Indeed, when Prince Rupert's cavaliers reached the outskirts of London late in 1642, Milton wrote and displayed on his door the sonnet 'Captain or Colonel, or Knight in Arms', not very courageously begging that his house might be spared as was the poet Pindar's when Alexander the Great captured Thebes in 335BC. In the event, the cavaliers were beaten back.

The years 1642–3 mark the end of what might be called Milton's first period, and the beginning of his second. From a personal point of view, his prolonged education was complete. Poetically, he had already

---

Milton's Prose Works, edited by C.R. Sumner, Bohn, London 1848–53 (hereafter referred to as Bohn), Vol. 1, pp.254–5.

written his early lyric poems: the 'Nativity Ode'; the companion poems 'L'Allegro' (the happy man) and 'Il Penseroso' (the serious man); the masque, *Comus*; the pastoral elegy, 'Lycidas'; and a number of sonnets, among them the autobiographical 'Twenty-Third Birthday' sonnet. Milton's second period is one of public office and political pamphleteering, with a few sonnets the only poetry. Then, with his blindness, comes the third period of personal defeat and disillusion, but the great days of his three long poems *Paradise Lost, Paradise Regained* and *Samson Agonistes*.

To return to the beginning of Milton's second period: in 1642 or 1643, Milton married Mary Powell, the daughter of a Royalist house with which his father had had business dealings; indeed, despite Mary's obvious physical attraction for Milton, this was primarily a marriage by arrangement, and was certainly no love match on her side. Mary speedily found the Puritan austerity and intellectual stature of her new husband too much for her, and promptly returned home. The war made reclamation difficult. This marriage is important because of the events it set in train. Had it not been for his own bitter personal experience, Milton would not have sought so vehemently to justify divorce by reference to scripture in four pamphlets. These pamphlets were condemned by theologians in Milton's own party, which was already, in 1643, severely limiting the licensing of books. Believing that two of his most strongly held principles were endangered—the right of individual interpretation of scripture and freedom of speech and writing—Milton in 1644 published *Areopagitica*, his noblest pamphlet, inspired by his love of liberty and free of the usual personal scurrility. His sympathies were now with the Cromwellian and army section of the Parliament side, with its greater religious tolerance, rather than with the austere Presbyterians who insisted on the doctrine of predestination and its consequent limitation of individual freedom. In 1649 Milton was made Latin Secretary to the Commonwealth with the official title of 'Secretary for the Foreign Tongues'; the revolutionary government used Latin as its language of diplomacy, and the learned Milton was a natural choice. His main tasks were to write pamphlets justifying government policy, particularly the execution of the King; to defeat the champions of the Royalist cause on paper; and to compose official despatches to the courts of Europe, from Stockholm to Savoy, for the victories of the English New Model Army had made Cromwell a man to be reckoned with in international relations.

By 1652 Milton had lost his sight completely, and in 1655 he was allowed a substitute Secretary. He now turned his mind back to poetry, though he continued to write anti-monarchical pamphlets until 1660, the year of the Restoration. Milton's third period, that of his long poems, coincides approximately with the first fourteen years of the Restoration

(1660–74), though there are grounds for believing that he wrote Satan's address to the sun (*Paradise Lost*, IV.32–113) as early as 1658. At the time of the Restoration, Milton as a well-known Cromwellian was in some physical danger, but the Royalist poet Davenant, placing poetry before politics, concealed him until the danger had passed. Henceforward Milton, blind, ailing and impoverished, lived quietly and unpersecuted in the midst of his triumphant enemies, visited by many friends and admirers, until his death in 1674.

Milton's relationships with his family are significant, though his view of the status of women affects *Paradise Lost* more in the books where Eve appears than in Books I and II. Relationships among the men in Milton's family were good; he loved his father deeply, and took him in and cared for him in his old age, addressing the poem 'Ad Patrem' to him; his nephews, the two brothers Phillips, continued to visit him after the Restoration, acted at times as his amanuenses (so necessary for a blind poet), and each wrote a memoir of him after his death. But he did not inspire love in women. His first wife, having left him soon after their marriage, was only reconciled to him when the Royalist cause was already lost; his three daughters were all her children. Four years after her death in childbirth, he married again, in 1656, only to lose his second wife in the same way; it is generally accepted that the sonnet 'Methought I saw my late espoused Saint' is dedicated to her, despite recent critical assertions that the only wife Milton ever 'saw' was his first. In his third period (he had a different wife in each), Milton married for a third time; it is difficult to avoid concluding that his main reason was to ease the housekeeping problems of a blind man. His daughters were made to read to him in languages they did not understand, and only the youngest, Deborah, spoke kindly of him after his death, and that when his reputation as a great poet was already established. The children, for their part, sought to cheat him out of the proceeds from his books. And yet Milton did not despise women. He thought the male partner should be predominant but a woman like Eve has grace and dignity to match Adam's male strength and intellect, and true wedded bliss such as we find in *Paradise Lost*, Book IV, comes from the perfect union of two different natures.

This divergence between precept and practice in his attitude to women is only one of the contradictions in Milton that make him so difficult to understand. A fervent lover of liberty and individual freedom, he for some time allied himself with Presbyterians who condemned free will; and he certainly did not believe in the basic equality of all men, regarding himself as set apart and destined for greatness, the chosen prophet of the new dispensation under which God intended Cromwellian England to teach the rest of Europe how to live. And his picture of Satan as the grand rebel against imposed authority, divine and benevolent though that authority may be, has caused the poets William Blake (1757–1827) and Percy Bysshe Shelley (1792–1822), to name but two, to maintain that Milton was of the Devil's party without knowing it.

Milton's cosmology

One further contradiction demands much fuller treatment—Milton's mixture of the two cosmologies, the Ptolemaic and the Copernican, in *Paradise Lost*. More far-reaching than the purely national quarrels between the King on the one hand and Parliament and the Puritans on the other, the changeover from the Ptolemaic to the Copernican system of cosmology affected the whole Western world; the poet John Donne (1571/2–1631) wrote with truth in the 'First Anniversary', 'And new Philosophy calls all in doubt'.

Throughout the Middle Ages it had been accepted that man was the centre of the universe and his earth the hub of a rotating planetary system. The seven known planets orbited the earth, each one's atmosphere pushing round the one next inside it by friction, thus creating a note of music; all the notes together made up the heavenly harmony, or music of the spheres. The outermost orbit, that of the planet Saturn, was itself surrounded by the sphere of the fixed stars (*Paradise Lost*, III.481) and outside that again was the vast expanse of the waters of the firmament, also called by Milton the Crystalline Sphere or the Hyaline (*Paradise Lost*, VII.619). These waters of the firmament, as distinct from the waters on the earth and under the earth, had been used by God as an insulating jacket designed to protect His newly-created universe from the excesses of cold and heat in the region of Chaos through which Satan flies at the end of Book II. The whole universe was suspended from heaven (also frequently called the Empyrean) by a golden chain (II.1051). In the area outside the Hyaline was the sphere of the *Primum Mobile*, or First Mover. This *Primum Mobile* transformed the love of God for mankind into energy and provided the impetus that made the whole universe rotate; the Middle Ages believed literally that it was Divine Love that made the world go round.

In heaven, God sat on His throne supported by four seraphim, the most powerful of the nine orders of angels which had remained loyal. The rebel tenth who had revolted under Satan had been hurled down into another dread realm, hell, created for them to occupy beyond the domain of Chaos and Old Night. How Satan breaks out of this prison of Hell, passing through the ninefold gates of adamant guarded by Sin and Death and winning his way through the abyss ruled by Chaos to reach the outer surface of our world takes up the second half of Book II of *Paradise Lost*.

Some of the features of this cosmology have been added to the Ptolemaic system as amended by Alfonso X of Castile in the thirteenth century: the golden chain on which the universe hangs, and the site and physical features of hell, for example. But the most interesting point about Milton's cosmology is this: why, when he knew of the discoveries Galileo had made with his telescope—as Book VIII clearly proves—and must have accepted the validity of the Copernican cosmology, which recognises that the sun and not the earth is the centre around which our planetary system revolves, did Milton base his universe upon the Ptolemaic pattern? The answer lies in the literary advantages of accepting the older though erroneous concept: it was known, and Copernicanism was strongly resisted and only slowly accepted; the Ptolemaic system was orderly, it laid down limits within which Milton found it easier to work; and it made God and man the two ends of a chain—man can ascend, onward and ever upward, to union with the divinity, and this could never have happened in an open-ended Copernican universe.

The epic

Paradise Lost is the only modern English representative of the epic genre; we exclude the so-called 'brief epic' represented by *Paradise Regained*.Epic itself is a very ancient form of poetry, originating in an age before writing, when long narratives dealing with the mighty deeds of the military aristocracy were recited to an assembled company, on long winter evenings or after a feasting. The narrative consisted of a series of loosely-linked and easily-detachable episodes—to enable the overall length to be varied as circumstances demanded—and centred on the exploits of some national hero who was something more than human if slightly less than divine, probably with one divine parent who helped him, argued his case in celestial councils, and endowed him with extraordinary qualities. To provide some rest for the reciter and some relief for the listeners, stock passages came to be included in the epic: the hero's ancestry; the description and history of his weapons; a council or debate, usually in heaven; and so on. These epics are called Primary Epics because their characteristics naturally reflect the society that gave them birth; and the most famous examples are the *Iliad* and the *Odyssey*, supposedly by the blind poet Homer, whose authorship and even existence are uncertain.

The main interest for readers of *Paradise Lost* lies in the Secondary Epic of the Roman poet Virgil (70–19BC). His great work, the *Aeneid*, was intended to be read by an individual in solitude, not recited to an assembly of listeners. The grandeur which had been natural to Primary Epic was artificially reproduced in Virgil by means of the conscious literary style of an individual artist, which the genealogies of weapons, long similies containing complete pictures in words, celestial councils and debates were imitated in a serious and lofty tone. Most remarkably, the character of the epic hero was altered to suit the changing spirit of the age. No longer is Achilles, seeking glory on the field of battle, the ideal; the Homeric-type hero in the *Aeneid*, Turnus, is defeated by a new ideal figure, Aeneas, still a hero with one divine and one mortal parent, still a brave and skilful fighter when the need arises, but also a more philosophical hero who must learn to control himself before he is judged fit to found an empire. These two elements, the consciously-created grand style and the hero who reflects the spirit of a new and more sophisticated age, were vital to Milton, as they must also be to any student of *Paradise Lost*.

The end of the fifteenth century saw the rise of another type of epic, the Romantic Epic of the Italian poets Ludovico Ariosto (1474–1533) and Matteo Maria Boiardo (1441?–94), characterised by exaggeration and, as its name implies, with no claim to historical truth. More significant were the Renaissance epics, in which the poets sought to do for their own countries what Virgil had done for Imperial Rome, and for their vernacular languages what Virgil had done for Latin. *Os Lusiadas*, by the Portuguese poet Luis de Camoëns (1524–80), published in 1572, is the best example of this type; it sings the praises of Vasco da Gama, the great Portuguese navigator, and actually begins with the same words as the *Aeneid*, 'Of arms and the man I sing'. Also of importance is the *Gerusalemme Liberata* by the late sixteenth-century Italian poet Torquato Tasso (1544–95) which deals with the liberation of Jerusalem in the Second Crusade—a religious subject of more than purely national interest; in this respect it resembles *Paradise Lost*.

The epic elements in *Paradise Lost*, Books I and II, will be discussed in the Commentary in Part 3, and the grandeur of Milton's style and the claims of Satan to be regarded as an epic hero considered. But here it is convenient to stress how Milton fits into the developing tradition. Determined to write some great work, he pondered over three problems: what literary form his great work should take; who was most suited to be its hero; and in what language it should be written. In the *Reason of Church Government* (1641), Milton lays his options clearly before us:

Time serves now now, and perhaps I might seem too profuse to give any certain account of what the mind at home, in the spacious circuits of her musing, hath liberty to propose to herself, though of highest hope and hardest attempting; whether that epic from whereof the two poems of Homer, and those other two of Virgil and Tasso, are a diffuse, and the book of Job a brief model: or whether the rules of Aristotle herein are strictly to be kept, or nature to be followed, which in them that know art, and use judgment, is no transgression, but an enriching of art: and lastly, what king or knight, before the conquest, might be chosen in whom to lay the pattern of a Christian hero. And as Tasso gave to a prince of Italy his choice whether he would command him to write of Godfrey's expedition against the Infidels, or Belisarius against the Goths, or Charlemain against the Lombards; if to the instinct of nature and the emboldening of art aught may be trusted, and that there be nothing adverse in our climate, or the fate of this age, it haply would be no rashness, from an equal diligence and inclination, to present the like offer in our own ancient stories; or whether those dramatic constitutions, wherein Sophocles and Euripides reign, shall be found more doctrinal and exemplary to a nation. The scripture also affords us a divine pastoral drama in the Song of Solomon, consisting of two persons, and a double chorus, as Origen rightly judges. And the Apocalypse of St John is the majestic image of a high and stately tragedy, shutting up and intermingling her solemn scenes and acts with a sevenfold chorus of hallelujahs and harping symphonies: and this my opinion the grave authority of Pareus, commenting that book, is sufficient to confirm. Or if occasion shall lead, to imitate those magnific odes and hymns, wherein Pindarus and Callimachus are in most things worthy, some others in their frame judicious, in their matter most an end faulty. But those frequent songs throughout the law and prophets beyond all these, not in their divine argument alone, but in the very critical art of composition, may be easily made appear over all the kinds of lyric poesy to be incomparable.*

Long epic, short epic, drama, pastoral and lyric are all here considered as possible forms, foreshadowing not merely *Paradise Lost* but *Paradise Regained* and *Samson Agonistes*; also 'the pattern of a Christian hero'. Milton's preference for scriptural literature over the classical, not only in subject but in style, may seem strange, but it is difficult to contradict him when he knew both languages and both literatures thoroughly and we do not. Eventually, Milton rejected the choice of a national hero, King Arthur, and a national subject, in favour of the universal subject of the Fall of Man. He chose the form of the long epic and, rejecting the general view that English was a shifting sand while Latin was lasting marble, decided, like a true Renaissance poet, to do for English what Virgil had done for Latin. 'I applied myself,' he wrote, 'to that resolution, which Ariosto followed against the persuasions of Bembo, to fix all the industry and art I could unite to the adorning of my native tongue.'*

*Bohn, Vol. 2, pp.478–9.
*Bohn, Vol. 2, p.478.

A note on the text

Every year in the decade beginning in 1652 has been put forward as the date when *Paradise Lost* was begun. All that is known for certain is that it was first published in 1667; but the assurance of the Quaker, Thomas Ellwood, who found Milton a cottage in the country during the Great Plague, that Milton gave him and manuscript to read at that time, may be accepted as evidence that the poem was complete by 1665. There was a second edition in 1674; Milton then divided the original Books VII and X into two each, thus making up the customary epic number of twelve. *Paradise Lost* continued to be admired and its elevated language imitated throughout the eighteenth century, and it did not lapse into oblivion with the Romantic Revival, for Wordsworth was one of Milton's greatest admirers. During the Victorian period *Paradise Lost* was one of the few books accepted as being suitable for Sunday reading, and the twentieth century has seen the publication of many editions. The Oxford Milton, Oxford University Press, London, 1904, revised 1969, contains the complete poems, without commentary or notes, but with the earliest possible spelling and punctuation, to which the blind and therefore sound-sensitive Milton paid such careful attention. The Milton volume edited by A. Fowler and J. Carey in the Longmans Annotated English Poets series, Longman, London, 1968, has a modernised text and is very fully and eruditely annotated. A.W. Verity's volume of notes to his own edition of *Paradise Lost*, Cambridge University Press, Cambridge, 1936, is still a valuable work of reference, and numerous paperback editions of two or more books of *Paradise Lost*, annotated and with critical introductions, have appeared since the end of World War II, designed to provide the necessary basic background for a study of Milton's text at a reasonable price.

Part 2

Summaries
of PARADISE LOST BOOKS I & II

A general summary

When the second edition of *Paradise Lost* was published in 1674, Milton added the *Arguments* which precede each book; these summarise the contents in the author's own words. The whole work is not one continuous narrative; in true Virgilian epic tradition, the story begins in the middle and earlier events are presented to the reader by various means—dreams, reminiscences and in conversations. Milton first states his general purpose, to tell the story of Man's fall; but we do not learn of the events leading up to this fall, and the consequences which stem from it, until much later. In Books V and VI, the seraph Raphael, sent down to Eden by God to enlighten and warn Adam, tells him of the revolt of Satan against God and how, inspired by pride, ambition and envy, he seduced one-tenth of the angelic host into following him. Summarily defeated by God's Son in a terrible war in heaven, Satan and his followers are hurled down to the place of fiery torment prepared for them, hell. Continuing his story in Book VII, Raphael tells Adam how the universe was created, culminating in the creation of man himself. Adam, having in Book VIII asked some questions on astronomy which reveal Milton's knowledge of Galileo's discoveries, proceeds to give his own version of his creation and that of Eve. With a final admonition on the value of Temperance, or self-control, Raphael departs. This means that the first acts of the drama actually take place in Books V–VIII.

After the initial statement of general purpose, Book I takes up the story of the rebel angels, newly arrived in hell, into which they have been hurled following their defeat in the war in heaven. Their situation, individual characters and occupations are described, and in Book II they meet in council to decide what is to be done. Finally, it is agreed that Satan shall fly off to the new world of man to see if he can strike at God through His new creation. Satan's escape from hell, his meeting with Sin and Death and his perilous passage to the surface of our world are then described.

In Book III the scene switches to heaven, where God delivers a long homily on man's freedom to choose between good and evil; complicated philosophical considerations of free will and predestination (Book III) and the doctrine of temperance (Book IX), vitally necessary as they are for a full understanding of Milton, do not immediately concern students of the first two Books. At the end of God's speech foreshadowing man's freely-chosen disobedience and fall, the Son offers Himself as the ransom for mankind and God accepts His sacrifice. Satan meanwhile has landed on the rim of the universe, and, finding his way in, flies down to the sun and thence to earth. In Book IV he observes the marital happiness of Adam and Eve and is aroused to a fury of envy. Uriel, regent of the sun, who has directed Satan on his way, observes his behaviour and reports back to Heaven. God sends Gabriel and an angelic patrol to Eden, and Satan is frustrated in his first attempt to tempt Eve by means of a dream and is expelled from Eden. God then sends Raphael, as we have seen, to alert Adam to the situation and to warn him. The warning is in vain as God had foreknown it would be, and in Book IX Milton changes his tone to tragic, claiming nevertheless that his theme is more truly heroic than the stories of classical and Romantic epic. Satan succeeds in his design of persuading Eve to taste the forbidden fruit, and Adam also eats, determined to share Eve's fate 'not deceived, but fondly overcome by female charm'. They become intemperate, first through lust and then through anger, blaming each other bitterly. Book X is a book of retribution and reconciliation. The Son comes down to Eden to pronounce God's sentence of expulsion, toil and mortality, tempered by the promise of ultimate victory over evil. Adam and Eve are reconciled and accept their fate with resignation. Satan meanwhile has not gone unpunished. Returning to hell in triumph, instead of the expected acclamation he is greeted by a universal hiss; for all his followers have become serpents, and he himself is forthwith transformed into the greatest serpent of them all.

The two concluding books of *Paradise Lost*, originally one, conform to another epic tradition, that of looking into the future; as Aeneas was permitted to foresee the Empire of Augustus (27BC–AD14), so Adam is shown a synopsis of Jewish history down to the redemption of mankind by Christ on the Cross. The first part, to the Flood, he is shown by the Archangel Michael in a vision (Book XI), but Michael relates the second part of the story (Book XII) to spare Adam's sight. Reconciled to his fate by the promise of ultimate redemption coming after so much evil, Adam takes Eve by the hand and they pass out of Eden to face the hardships of the outside world together.

Detailed summaries

Book I, lines 1–26

In true epic manner, Milton begins by stating his general purpose—to demonstrate how justly and benevolently God has dealt with man before, during and after his fall—and by invoking the aid of a heavenly rather than an epic muse to elevate his style to match the greatness of his design.

NOTES AND GLOSSARY:

lines 1–16: In one long sentence, Milton states his epic purpose; but the justification of God's ways to man, even if 'justify' in the Latin sense of 'demonstrate' is accepted, can hardly be claimed as the central theme. Neither God nor man plays any significant part in Books I and II

Of: concerning (Latin: *de*)

that forbidden tree: the tree of knowledge (see the Bible, Genesis 2.17)

mortal: deadly

one greater Man: Jesus Christ, the 'second Adam'

Restore: is future tense; 'will redeem'

seat: abode, as in 'country seat'

heavenly Muse: It was customary in classical epic to invoke the aid of a Muse, one of the nine responsible for the arts and science. Milton invokes a heavenly Muse called Urania, 'the Heavenly One', in VII.1–7. Not to be confused with the classical Muse of astronomy of the same name

secret: covered by cloud and smoke (see the Bible, Exodus 19.16–18)

Oreb ... Sinai: Milton refers to biblical mountains in preference to Olympus, Helicon, or Parnassus; Horeb, where Moses saw the burning bush (Exodus 3), and Sinae, where God gave him the Ten Commandments (Exodus 19.20)

shepherd: Moses

chosen seed: the Children of Israel

lines 10–12: Milton once more parallels classical epic. Instead of the spring Aganippe which rises by the altar of Zeus and was the home of the Muses, he refers to Siloa, a spring and a pool close by Mount Zion

oracle of God: the Temple on Mount Moriah, outside Jerusalem. Siloa was in the valley nearby

no middle flight: Milton intends his poem to have both sublimity of subject and grandeur of style. Medieval rhetoricians recognised three levels of style, of which Milton rejects the middle (*medians*) in favour of the highest (*sublimis*)

Aonian mount: Helicon in Greece, sacred to the classical Muses

pursues:	deals with
Spirit:	the Holy Spirit, third person of the Trinity. Christian theology is not very clear as to its exact nature, and Milton thinks of it as similar though superior to his heavenly Muse
Dove-like:	In the Bible, Luke 3.22, the Holy Spirit descends upon Jesus 'in bodily form, as a dove'. Milton imagines it here as participating in the creation
dark:	'ignorant' rather than 'blind'
highth:	this is the form normally used by Milton
argument:	subject
assert:	vindicate
justify:	demonstrate, explain

Book I, lines 27–298

Satan: his appearance is described and his character revealed in dialogue with his chief lieutenant, Beelzebub. His pre-eminence and pride, even in defeat, are stressed—beaten in battle he may have been, but his determination is unshaken; nor is he deterred by the horrors of his new abode. Rousing himself, he makes his way to the shore of the burning lake. Armed like an epic hero, he rallies his broken legions.

NOTES AND GLOSSARY:

Say:	Milton is here addressing his heavenly Muse
tract:	area, expanse
grand parents:	original ancestors, Adam and Eve
fall off:	desert
For one restraint:	on account of the single prohibition not to eat of the tree of knowledge
besides:	in everything else
what time:	at the time when
peers:	equals
trusted:	confidently anticipated
the most High:	Hebrew ephithet for God, 'Elohim'
ethereal sky:	heaven
ruin:	falling (Latin: *ruina*)
combustion:	destruction by fire. Luke 10.18: 'I saw Satan fall like lightning from heaven'
adamantine:	an adjective usually applied to impenetrably hard rock or precious stones; 'abnormally strong'
fiery gulf:	burning lake of hell
his doom:	the judgement passed on Satan; compare 'doomsday' (Day of Judgement), as in *Doomsday Book*

line 55:	The rebel angels had not known *pain* before their fall
baleful:	malevolent
as far as angels' ken:	to the full extent of an angel's superhuman range of vision
discover:	reveal
shades:	places of shadow
sulphur:	brimstone (see the Bible, Revelation 19.20; 20.10)
line 74:	The distance between hell and heaven is three times the distance from the centre of the universe (earth) to the point at its outer extremity nearest to the empyrean
Beelzebab:	Baal-zebab, 'lord of the flies', a local manifestation of the pagan god Baal worshipped as a sun-god by the Philistines in Palestine
thence:	because the Hebrew word 'Satan' means 'the adversary'
He:	God
injured merit:	Satan's revolt was inspired by envy of the Son (see V.662–5)
adverse:	contrary
dubious:	of uncertain result. The battle lasted for three days
field:	battlefield
study:	planning of, pursuit of
lines 108–11	Uncertainty in the punctuation has led to confusion in interpreting these lines. According to the second edition of 1674, line 108 should be followed by a colon, 109 by a question mark, with a full stop after 'me' in 111. Thus 109 means 'and what else is there to not being overcome than this?'
Doubted:	This is not true: the issue of the war in heaven was never in doubt. But Satan is the father of lies, and even his most ringing rhetoric lacks truth of substance
by fate:	Satan recognises the supremacy of Fate, not God
empyreal substance:	the heavenly matter of which the immortal angels are made
more successful hope:	greater hope of success
line 124:	God is a tyrant to Satan, not to Milton
apostate:	one who has changed sides (by implication from good to bad), particularly in religious beliefs
throned powers:	a reference to angels in general, not to the order of angels called Thrones; see note on 'Cherub', p.20
line 133:	Beelzebub also denies that God is the ultimate source of authority in the world

essences:	beings
extinct:	extinguished. This is an absolute construction on the Latin model
Of force:	perforce
entire:	unimpaired. Beelzebub suggests that God has left him their strength so that they may withstand pain better and work harder for Him as slaves
suffice:	suffer
To undergo:	so that we may undergo
Cherub:	The cherubim were second in the orders of angels to the seraphim, but Milton is inclined to call them all 'archangels' on occasion, though the archangels were only the eighth order. The nine orders, or trinal triplicities of three times three, the most magic of numbers, were: 1. Seraphim; 2. Cherubim; 3. Thrones / 4. Dominions; 5. Princedoms or Principalities; 6. Powers / 7. Virtues; 8. Archangels; 9. Angels
Doing or suffering:	whether active or passive. The Middle Ages respected the contemplative life as a preparation for the after-life, but Milton, as he shows in *Areopagitica* ('I cannot praise a fugitive and cloistered virtue') (Bohn, Vol. 2, p.68), was a strong exponent of the superiority of the active life
if I fail not:	if I am not mistaken
ministers:	those who administered
his:	Milton avoids using 'its', which had only recently (*c*.1600) come into use as a neuter possessive pro-noun
slip the occasion:	miss the opportunity
tend:	make our way
afflicted powers:	beaten troops (Latin: *afflictus*, routed)
offend:	strike back at
lines 190–1:	If they can find no encouragement in hope, they can at least strengthen their resolution by despair. Hope is a Christian virtue, absolute despair the ultimate sin, since it implies lack of faith in God
rood:	quarter of an acre; a unit of square measure
As whom:	one of the formulas used by Milton to introduce an epic simile
fables:	classical myths, contemptuously called fables by Milton to distinguish them from Christian truth. He was nevertheless deeply learned in classical mythology, and used it extensively in his poetry

lines 198–200:	The exact details of the earliest Greek mythology are understandably confused, and Titans and Giants are sometimes indistinguishable. Uranus (the sky) had three gigantic and hundred-handed children by Ge (the earth), of whom Briareus was one. He drove them out and fathered a second set of children, the Titans, whom Ge encouraged to make war upon him. The Titan Cronos, or Saturn, became ruler of the universe, to be driven out in turn by his son Zeus, the Roman Jove. Meanwhile Ge had borne a brood of giants, serpents and monsters to Tartarus (the underworld); one of them was Typhon, who had his lair in Tarsus, capital of Cilicia in Asia Minor. The Giants warred unsuccessfully against Zeus, and were imprisoned under volcanoes
Leviathan:	any huge monster, but here identified by Milton with the whale
pilot:	the master of the vessel, who would take the wheel himself in difficult conditions
night-foundered:	benighted, prevented by darkness from continuing its voyage
lee:	the sheltered side
Invests:	covers as with a garment
heaved:	lifted
line 212:	This 'high permission' for Satan to work evil presents Milton with a difficult problem, and his explanations are not entirely convincing
reiterated:	often repeated
Infinite goodness:	the redemption of mankind by Jesus Christ
incumbent:	leaning his weight on
And such:	substances such as volcanic ash. It was believed that sudden blasts of underground wind caused volcanoes to erupt; an example is Etna, in Sicily, with Pelorus (now Cape Faro) nearby to the north-east. An epic simile
Sublimed with mineral fury:	with the solid contents of the earth beneath the volcano changed into gushing liquid fire
bottom:	hollow, crater
involved:	wreathed in
resting:	a resting-place
Stygian:	Styx is one of the four rivers of hell
supernal:	divine
clime:	climate

change for:	possess instead of
sovereign:	habitually spelt 'sovran' by Milton to indicate the desired disyllabic pronunciation; derived from Italian *sovrano* as opposed to the more customary French *souverain*
dispose and bid:	arrange and order. Satan argues that by rights he is God's equal; only superior strength has given God the victory and with it the power to impose His will
happy fields:	the Elysian Fields, according to Greek mythology the happy home of virtuous souls after death
all but less than:	nearly equal to; a confused construction
lines 259–260:	God will not envy Satan his new and horrible kingdom
astonished:	thunderstruck, dazed
oblivious pool:	pool of forgetfulness, though not to be confused with the river Lethe (see II.583)
mansion:	dwelling place
liveliest pledge:	most certain assurance
edge:	front line
Grovelling:	flat on their faces (Middle English: *gruf*)
such a pernicious highth:	so great and dangerous a distance
ponderous:	heavy. Earlier epics contain long descriptions of the hero's equipment: the shield of Achilles in *Iliad*, XIX.23; the lances in *Gerusalemme Liberata*, VI.40
Ethereal temper:	made in heaven
optic glass:	telescope
Tuscan artist:	Galileo (1564–1642), whom Milton visited during his Italian tour in 1638. Fiesole is on a hill three miles from Florence, which is in the valley of the river Arno. Galileo was the first man to observe the moon's surface through a telescope with sufficient clarity to distinguish such features as spots
ammiral:	flagship. Again, as in 'sovran' above, Milton prefers the Italian word *ammiraglia* for its sound-value
marl:	ground; usually 'rich soil'

Book I, lines 299–587

The fallen angels are listed in great detail. Milton equates them with the false gods of scripture and the classics, thus making them more comprehensible in human terms to his readers.

NOTES AND GLOSSARY:

Natheless:	nevertheless; already archaic in Milton's time

Vallambrosa:	the 'valley of the shade', a leafy valley near Florence. An epic simile
Etrurian:	Tuscan. Florence is in Tuscany
embower:	make leafy bowers
sedge:	The Hebrew name for the Red Sea is Yam Suf, the Sea of Sedge, on account of the large amount of seaweed in it. Storms which coincide with the rising of the constellation of Orion tear up large quantities of this weed, which floats on the surface of the sea. The comparison is particularly apt
line 307:	Mention of the Red Sea recalls the safe passage of the children of Israel through it, and the subsequent destruction of Pharaoh and his pursuing forces (Exodus 14.28). The Hebrews had lived as slaves in Goshen, and Pharaoh is called 'perfidious' because he had let them go and then changed his mind. There is no record that this particular Pharaoh was named Busiris, and this, along with Milton's use of 'Memphian chivalry' (from Memphis on the Nile) instead of 'Egyptian cavalry', points to this line being one of those in which Milton indulges his love of resounding proper names
Abject:	thrown down
virtue:	valour (Latin: *virtus*)
linked thunderbolts:	used by Zeus against the rebel Giants; see note to lines 198–200 above
wont:	accustomed
Amram's son:	Moses, who called down a plague of locusts upon Egypt with his rod (Exodus 10.12–15). An epic simile
coast:	land
warping:	moving to and fro
cope:	canopy
lines 351–5:	The fallen angels, having in their great numbers been compared to a carpet of leaves when lying down and a swarm of locusts when in flight, are now likened on the ground to the barbarian hordes invading Rome. The invasions of the Goths, the Vandals and the Huns, together covering the period AD408–53, originated in the east rather than in the north, though they did cross the Rhine and the Danube, and the Vandals penetrated into North Africa and founded an empire there
erst:	formerly

new names: The fallen angels, having lost the names by which they were formerly known in heaven, are given the names by which they were later to be known on earth, those of pagan gods and idols

high sufferance: divine permission. The fallen angels were allowed to be worshipped as heathen deities as part of God's plan for the testing of mankind

gay religions: colourful rituals. Milton and his fellow Puritans abhorred pomp and ceremony in religion

for deities: as gods

who first: this long catalogue of the devils' leaders is in the epic manner; it parallels the list of Homer's warriors and their ships in *Iliad*, II.484–877

promiscuous crowd: the horde of nameless devils, unworthy of individual mention

The chief: reserved for Milton's first and strongest attack are those pagan gods who seduced the Israelites from the worship of Jehovah

line 384: Manasseh set up altars to heathen gods in the Temple (see the Bible, 2 Kings 21.4)

Jehovah thundering: as in Exodus 20, when giving the Ten Commandments to Moses

the cherubim: the golden figures at either end of the ark in the Temple (see the Bible, Psalm 80.1)

Abominations: idolatries

Moloch: means 'king'. Moloch was a sun-god, worshipped by the children of Ammon with human sacrifice (see 2 Kings 23.10). Milton here closely follows the details in Sandys's *Relation of a Journey* (1637 edition), which describes on page 186 how the priests of Moloch blew trumpets and clanged cymbals to drown the shrieks of the children being burned in the idol's hollow belly

lines 397–9: These places were all east of the Jordan, and the river Arnon was the boundary between Moab and the Amorites

fraud: guile. Misled by some of his many foreign wives, the wise king Solomon built a temple to Moloch on the Mount of Olives and dedicated a grove to him in the valley of Hinnom, part of the royal gardens. When Josiah reformed Jerusalem (see 2 Kings 23.10), he turned the grove into a rubbish dump, and it was known thereafter as Tophet and Gehenna, also names for hell

type:	prototype, model
Chemos:	god of the Moabites, known by different names (for instance, Peor) in different localities. To him also Solomon raised a temple, persuaded to do so by his foreign wives
lines 407–11:	The places named are in Moab, south-east of the Dead Sea, the 'Asphaltic Pool', so called because of the bituminous scum floating on it. Heshbon was the city of Sihon, king of the Amorites, who had formerly conquered the Moabites (see the Bible, Numbers 21.26). Milton spells proper names without an 'h' where possible—Basan, Chemos, Hesebon, Seon, Sittim; but Thammuz for its softer sound
Peor:	the name by which the Israelites worshipped Chemosh when they passed through Shittim in the land of Moab soon after leaving Egypt
orgies:	rites
enlarged:	spread. Originally worshipped in Shittim as a local manifestation of Chemosh, Peor became one of the gods revered in Jerusalem by Solomon
hill of scandal:	the temples built by Solomon for Moloch and Chemosh on the Mount of Olives were destroyed by Josiah (2 Kings 23.13). This iconoclasm made Josiah a great favourite with the Puritans
lines 419–21:	The land between the river Euphrates on the north-eastern border of Syria—probably called 'old' because mentioned in the Bible as early as Genesis 2—and the river Besor on the boundary of Egypt
Baalim:	the local gods of Palestine
Ashtaroth:	moon-goddesses, of whom Ashtoreth (line 438 below) was one
lines 424–31:	The fallen angels retain the ability to assume any shape they please, or either sex, for their essence is unmixed ('uncompounded') with any other element in the way a human spirit is contained in a body. In the course of the poem, Satan himself assumes many different shapes

Dilated or condensed: expanded or contracted
Their living strength: the true God
in troop: in a body

Astoreth:	a moon-goddess, also known as Astarte; hence her 'crescent horns' and title 'queen of heaven'
line 441:	Sidon was for a time the chief city of Phoenicia

uxorious king:	Solomon who, despite his wisdom and his 'large heart' (see 1 Kings 4.29), allowed his over-fondness for women to mislead him into raising altars to false gods (see 1 Kings 11.1–8). The Mount of Olives is called 'offensive' (and 'opprobrious' in line 403 above) because of the purpose for which it was used
Thammuz:	a fertility sun-god, equivalent of the Greek Adonis, who was, according to myth, slain on Mount Lebanon by a boar. He was mourned annually in Babylon when the plants died in the summer heat, while in Phoenicia the maidens bewailed his death each spring when the river Adonis in spate carried the red mud down from Mount Lebanon. The ritual must have spread to Israel, for Ezekiel saw in a vision the women 'weeping for Tammuz' at the north gate of the Temple (see the Bible, Ezekiel 8.14)
supposed:	supposedly
alienated Judah:	the tribe of Judah had turned away from God
lines 457–66:	Dagon, a fish-god or corn-god, was worshipped by the Philistines who lived to the south-west of Jerusalem, and is the best known of the pagan gods of the Old Testament by reason of the stories of David and Goliath and of Samson. The Philistines defeated the Israelites in battle and, when the latter brought the ark of the Lord from Shiloh to strengthen Jewish morale, the Philistines captured it and placed it in Dagon's temple (see the Bible, 1 Samuel 5.1–4). Next morning the image of Dagon had fallen down and, when raised up again, it was found on the following morning face downward on the threshold with its hands and head broken off. The five places mentioned are the five principal cities of the Philistines
in earnest:	as opposed to the ritual mourning for Thammuz
grunsel:	groundsel, threshold
lines 467–76:	Rimmon was a sun-god worshipped in Syria, the land between the two rivers Abana and Pharpar with its capital at Damascus, famous for its roses. The story of Namaan, the leper cured by Elisha and consequently converted, is told in 2 Kings 5; and that of King Ahaz, who caused a copy of Rimmon's altar in Damascus to be set up in the Temple in Jerusalem, is told in 2 Kings 16.10–16

sottish:	foolish—because he allowed himself to be overcome by the god he had conquered
drew:	caused
lines 477–482:	The divinities of ancient Egypt are scornfully called a 'crew' by Milton. Their chief god Osiris, was worshipped in the form of a sacred bull, Isis as a cow, and her son Horus, the sun-god, as a hawk
monstrous:	of animals
abused:	deceived
wandering:	According to the Roman poet Ovid (43BC–AD18) in *Metamorphoses*, V.319–31, the gods of Olympus fled from the giant Typhoeus into Egypt, where they lived in the forms of animals and later came to be worshipped by the Egyptians
lines 482–4:	Israel did not escape this animal-worship; the most famous instance is the making of the golden calf while Moses was away receiving the Commandments
lines 484–9:	Ten of the twelve tribes of Israel deserted Rehoboam, son of Solomon, leaving him only Judah and Benjamin, and turned to Jeroboam, 'the rebel king', who had been in Egypt. Jeroboam set up two golden calves, one in Bethel and one in Dan, and told the people that Jehovah in the form of an ox-god had slain the first-born of the Egyptians and led his people out of bondage (see 1 Kings 12.28–9)
equalled:	by destroying them
all her bleating gods:	Milton pours scorn on animal images
lines 490–505:	Belial is the personification of intemperance through lust, to Milton the greatest enemy of all; through it both Adam and Samson were to fall. The fact that Belial has no temple nor recognisable image makes him all the more dangerous; he can appear anywhere. In the Old Testament, the Sons of Eli the high priest seduced the maidservants in the Temple itself, while the sexual perversion to which Sodom gave its name (see Genesis 19) was only avoided in Gibeah by the traveller offering the rapists his concubine (see the Bible, Judges 19.16–30). Milton also may have had in mind here the lechery of the Restoration court and the insecurity of London's streets after dark
flown:	high, as if on drugs
prime:	foremost

lines 508-21: Despite his great debt to the classics, Milton regards the Greek gods as inferior even to the Old Testament idols because they were created after heaven and earth, from whom in their forms of Uranus and Ge the Greeks themselves claimed their gods to be descended. Milton, following the Bible (Genesis 10), derives the Greek race from Javan, grandson of Noah, thus making them a cadet branch of the Hebrew nation. He sketches the history of the heavenly hierarchy of Greece (see notes to 198–200 above). The Titans under Cronos or Saturn seized supreme power from Uranus; he was superseded in turn by his son Zeus or Jove, encouraged by his mother, Rhea. The worship of Saturn nevertheless spread westwards across the Adriatic into Italy, and beyond to the Celtic races in the extreme west of Europe. Meanwhile Zeus, raised in secret on mount Ida in Crete, had established his power on Mount Olympus in north-eastern Greece. Milton comments that this was the nearest to heaven the Greek gods ever reached; but their worship extended throughout Greece, the 'Doric land', with an oracle of Zeus at Dodona and the more famous one of Apollo at Delphi

the middle air: God allowed the fallen angels to control 'the middle air', the region in which storms were generated. Satan in *Paradise Regained*, IV, seeks to intimidate Christ by a thunderstorm

utmost isles: Britain

damp: depressed in spirit

Obscure: not immediately apparent. The fallen angels are encouraged by Satan's defiant appearance, while he is momentarily discouraged by their dejection

straight: immediately

clarion: a small war-trumpet

Azazel: according to Hebrew tradition, Azazel was the leader of the evil angels who seduced the daughters of men (see Genesis 6)

advanced: upraised

emblazed: emblazoned, heraldically decorated

universal host: entire assembly

concave: vaulted roof of rock

reign: the realm of Chaos, from a part of which God had created hell to receive the defeated rebel angels

orient:	bright
serried:	locked together
anon:	forthwith
phalanx:	battle formation perfected by the Macedonians and contributing to Alexander the Great's conquests; here referring to the Spartans (Dorians), who marched into battle to the music of flutes. The 'Dorian mode' was intended to inspire its hearers with steadfast courage, as opposed to the softer and more effeminate Lydian mode. Milton was an accomplished musician
wanting:	lacking
swage:	assuage
Advanced in view:	they have now changed formation and are in open order ready to be reviewed
horrid front:	a line of bristling spears (Latin: *horridus*)
in guise of:	with the appearance of
ordered:	military term meaning held outwards from the body with the right hand and with the butt resting on the ground
traverse:	from end to end
sums:	adds up
lines 573–88:	If all the most celebrated armies since the creation were joined together, they could not compare in numbers and courage with the embattled array of fallen angels. The beginning of a series of epic similes, cumulative in their effect
small infantry:	the pygmies, to whom all the heroic hosts of fact and fiction, classical and Romantic, are compared
giant brood:	the Giants who fought against the Olympian gods at Phlegra in Macedonia
line 578:	The two best-known conflicts of ancient Greece were the Trojan War and Seven against Thebes, in which even the gods lent their aid. The fight of the Seven Argive Heroes at Thebes is the subject of a tragedy by Aeschylus (525–456BC)
Uther's son:	King Arthur, surrounded by knights from Great and Little Britain (Brittany, Latin: *Armorica*). To Milton, King Arthur represented one of the great sources of medieval chivalric tales, the Matter of Britain; Charlemagne another, the Matter of France; while all the classical myths and legends were grouped together as the Matter of Rome the Great

lines 582–7:	Milton indulges his fondness for resounding proper names to the full here. The place-names are taken from the Italian Romantic epics *Orlando Innamorato* by Boiardo and its continuation by Ariosto, *Orlando Furioso*, (published in 1532) though the defeat of Charlemagne's rearguard at Roncesvalles was well known from the *Chanson de Roland*, the twelfth-century *Chanson de geste*, or French historical verse romance. 'Fontarabbia' is probably chosen by Milton in place of Roncesvalles for its sound-value and falling cadence

Book I, lines 588–669

Satan's pre-eminence stressed: he addresses his assembled legions, spurring them to continued defiance; what they must now determine is the best way to organise renewed resistance to God

NOTES AND GLOSSARY:

her:	its
lines 594–6:	When the newly-risen sun shines horizontally through the atmosphere, it loses its beams, as Satan has lost his halo. An epic simile
lines 597–9:	Eclipses were supposed to presage disaster, particularly a change of king. These three lines narrowly escaped being cut by the censor of the first edition
considerate:	thoughtful
cast:	shed (tears)
amerced:	deprived
scathed:	damaged
event:	results
dire:	calamitous
puissant:	powerful
counsels different:	failure to abide by an agreed plan. Satan strongly denies that either independent action or avoidance of danger on his part contributed to their defeat
old repute:	long-standing tradition
regal state:	trappings of absolute rule
part:	course of action
Space:	used in its modern sense of outer space
fame:	rumour (Latin: *fama*)
eruption:	exploratory sally out of hell
understood:	undeclared
highly:	emotionally

Book I, lines 670–798

Hell is made habitable by the fallen angels under Mammon's direction, and a place prepared for the vital council which Satan has convened. As the book ends, the leaders of the rebels assemble in Pandæmonium to begin their great debate on ways and means.

NOTES AND GLOSSARY:

grisly:	horrible
lines 671–674:	The hillside was covered with flakes of sulphurous substances. Metal ores were thought to be the product of sulphur and quicksilver subjected to heat underground
cast:	throw up
least erected:	Unlike the other creatures, angelic or human, whose reason reaches upward to God, Mammon, even while still in heaven, had cast his eyes down and debased his thoughts to material riches
else:	otherwise
vision beatific:	the sight of God
centre:	centre of the earth
ribs:	seams (of ore)
admire:	be surprised (Latin: *admiror*, to wonder at)
precious bane:	an oxymoron, not merely of sense (precious yet deadly), but also of language origin (Latin: *pretiosus*, and Old English: *bana*, a slayer)
line 694:	The Tower of Babel and the Egyptian pyramids are small achievements in comparison
art:	craftsmanship
reprobate:	cast off by God
Sluiced:	conducted by means of sluices
founded:	melted, as in a foundry
Severing:	separating out
bullion dross:	the scum on the liquid metal
various:	complex
strange conveyance:	an ingenious method of conducting
exhalation:	mist, illusion. Like the machinery of a Jacobean masque, the palace of Pandæmonium rises, on classical architectural lines, to the accompaniment of music
symphonies:	melodies harmonising with the voices
lines 713–17:	'pilasters' are inset square pillars; 'round' therefore means 'around, in a circle'. 'Doric pillars' are one of three basic classical designs, the others being Ionic

	and Corinthian; the 'architrave' is the main beam resting on top of a row of pillars, the 'frieze' is immediately above it, and the 'cornice' tops the whole
want:	lack
bossy:	in relief
fretted:	in decorative patterns, usually made up of straight lines
lines 717–22:	Babylon, the centre of the worship of the Assyrian god Baal, and Memphis, here called Alcairo, where there was a temple dedicated to Apis the calf-god, are cited as types of heathen splendour
pile:	edifice
Pendent:	suspended
cressets:	iron brackets containing lumps of blazing asphalt
naphtha:	inflammable liquid used in lamps
line 737:	The nine orders of angels were divided into a hierarchy of three sets of three, the trinal triplicities; the seraphim were the highest and the angels the lowest (see note on 'Cherub', p.20)
lines 738–51:	Ausonia is the Greek name for Italy, and Mulciber is Hephæstus, or Vulcan. Milton denies the truth of the story that Vulcan was thrown out of Olympus by Zeus and landed, crippled, on the island of Lemnos in the Aegean, claiming that he fell long before with Satan
engines:	inventions, contrivances
industrious crew:	workers
Pandæmonium:	assembly of all the demons; from the Greek
place or choice:	importance or election
lines 763–66:	A parenthetic reference to the jousts held between individual crusaders and Saracens, sometimes to the death, sometimes just to the breaking of a single lance
soldan:	sultan
paynim:	pagan
Taurus:	the second sign of the zodiac. The sun passes through it in spring, between mid-April and mid-May
line 772–5:	A smooth plank led into the entrance of the hive, which would be thatched with straw; it was rubbed with balm to attract the bees
expatiate and confer:	walk about discussing
straitened:	packed; but they reduce their size by magic to give themselves more room

Indian mount:	the Himalayas, on the other side of which pygmies were believed to live
arbitress:	overseer of the elfin revels
jocund:	merry and sprightly
close recess and secret conclave: secret council. Milton may be repeating himself in order to satirise the conclave by which Roman Catholic cardinals elect a new Pope	
Frequent:	numerous
summons read:	the authority on which the meeting had been called having been read out
consult:	consultation, debate

Book II

In summary, Book II is divisible into three distinct sections:

1. The great debate, itself split up into the various speeches.
2. The occupations of the fallen angels in hell during Satan's absence.
3. Satan's voyage.

Book II, lines 1–42

Satan opens the great council of fallen angels. He first asserts his own right to leadership on three counts: appointment by heavenly law and title; free choice; his own merit. He stresses his unenviable position as leader, for he will be first to suffer from God's greater vengence if they fail. He calls for expressions of opinion.

NOTES AND GLOSSARY:

lines 2–4:	The richness of Satan's state far surpasses the wealth of Ormuz, an island in the Persian Gulf famous for its jewels, or of India, scene of Camoëns' epic, *Os Lusiadas* (see p.12)
barbaric:	oriental
by merit:	Satan had become supreme in evil by desert, not by inheritance or election—though this he later claims
success:	result, not necessarily favourable
Powers and Dominions: two of the nine orders of angels (see note on 'Cherub', p.20)	
virtues:	a play upon words; added to 'heavenly qualities', it glances at another order of angels, the Virtues
line 16:	Much of the evil in *Paradise Lost* is a grim parody of the good. This idea of purification by trial is an oft-repeated Miltonic doctrine; see the passage from *Areopagitica* quoted on p.55 below

lines 18–24:	Satan justifies his right to lead the rebel angels: he was their superior in heaven; he had been divinely appointed; they themselves had chosen him; he had shown his superiority in council and on the battlefield; and now no one could envy him his preeminence in torment
lines 24–5:	The state of affairs in heaven, based on the hierarchy of the nine orders, could, on the other hand, breed envy
faction:	dissident groups
Surer to prosper:	because things can only get better

Book II, lines 43–105

Moloch speaks first, proposing an immediate renewal of hostilities. What worse can befall them if they fail? If they are immortal, no pains can be greater than those they now suffer. And if they can be and are utterly destroyed, oblivion is better than their present state. Also, they can inflict a lot of damage before they are beaten.

NOTES AND GLOSSARY:

sceptered:	Homer gives his king this epic epithet
recked:	cared
thereafter:	most editors render 'accordingly', in keeping with his character; but 'thereupon' is also possible
sentence:	vote
unexpert:	inexperienced
horrid:	frightful. The horrors of hell should be used to attack heaven
engine:	the chariot of wrath used by the Son in their expulsion from heaven; see VI.749–59
Tartarean:	hellish. Milton equates hell with the classical underworld
such:	those who think the way both difficult and steep
drench:	large dose, usually given to animals
forgetful lake:	see I.266
proper motion:	the natural movement of a spiritual being upwards. Not being subject to the laws of gravity, the rebel angels did not fall; they had to be driven downwards
laborious:	difficult because unnatural
event:	result, outcome
exercise:	occupy. Moloch here uses the terminology of religious discipline

what doubt we to incense: why do we hesitate to arouse?

essential:	spiritual essence
lines 100–1:	We are already in the worst possible state this side of annihilation

---

Book II, lines 106–228

Next, the smooth-tongued Belial counsels acceptance of their present state: are they not free to meet in council? Even though they suffer pain, they exist and they can think, and such gifts should not be thrown away by renewal of the war—not that such a renewal would be allowed by God to take place, nor could it harm Him even if it did. By keeping a low profile the fallen angels may persuade God to commute their sentence and ease their torments, which will, in any case, seem less terrible as they become familiar.

NOTES AND GLOSSARY:

dangerous:	destructive
in act more humane:	more polished in manner
manna:	words as sweet as honey
dash:	confound. Belial is depicted as a sophist, able by specious reasoning to make the worst course of action seem the best; he demolishes Moloch's argument point by point
success:	result, as in line 9 above
fact:	feat
scope:	aim, end
watch:	guards, sentries
obscure wing:	unpredictable patrols
could we:	even if we could
ethereal mould:	what God is made of
Her:	its, referring to 'insurrection'
intellectual being:	existence with the power to think. Compare the statement by the French philosopher René Descartes (1596–1650), *cogito, ergo sum*, 'I think, therefore I exist'
sense:	the power of feeling
Let:	accepting that
Belike through impotence:	through impatience, perhaps. Said sarcastically
Wherefore cease we:	why should we give up the struggle and accept annihilation?
amain:	with all speed
intermitted:	the pursuing fire had stopped, for the time being at least (see I.172)

red right hand:	a direct translation of the description of Jupiter by the Roman poet Horace (65–8BC)
firmament:	roof
Impendent:	hanging over our heads
racking:	torturing, as on the rack
converse:	dwell with
Unrespited:	without relief
With:	(achieve) against
motions:	proposals, plans
thus vile:	reduced to this miserable state
lines 199–203:	Had we been wise, we should have made up our minds to suffer the consequences of failure, recognising the power of our enemy and the possibility of defeat
those:	Moloch and his sympathisers
remit:	reduce
line 212:	Will not think about us if we keep passive
inured:	having become accustomed to
Familiar:	as normal. Accustomed to their hellish environment, the devils will no longer feel any pain
lines 224–5:	We may be worse off than we were, but things are not as bad as they might be—and will surely be if we invite further vengeance

---

Book II, lines 229–98

Mammon follows, dismissing armed resistance as futile and passive acceptance of their fate as alien to their natures and convictions. He proposes that the fallen angels should henceforward accept hell as their natural environment, adapt themselves to its conditions, develop its resources, and build an independent, orderly and fiery empire. His proposal is greeted with loud acclaim.

NOTES AND GLOSSARY:

when:	that is, never
strife:	between Fate and Chance
former:	to disenthrone God
latter:	to regain our lost rights
warbled:	a contemptuous description
ambrosial:	fragrant. Ambrosia was the food of the gods
lines 250–1:	What is impossible to gain by force and undesirable to gain by God's permission
recess:	remote area where the fallen angels make themselves self-sufficient

Wants:	lacks
our elements:	our natural environment
sensible:	sensation; adjective used as a noun
invite:	point towards
Compose:	arrange
o'erwatched:	exhausted by being too long on watch
field:	battlefield
Michael:	(pronounced here with three syllables) the captain of God's army in the war in heaven. His two-handed sword is described in VI.250–3
nether:	lower, meaning in hell
policy:	cunning statesmanship

Book II, lines 299–389

The general enthusiasm for Mammon's plan does not suit Satan and Beelzebub, who have already decided what is best to be done. Making full use of his powers of oratory and the respect in which he is widely held, Beelzebub points out that God would never permit the establishment of a rival empire. Attack he favours, but not direct attack. He tells the assembled devils about the new world God has created and the new race of men destined to inhabit it. This new world will be less strongly guarded than heaven, and may be destroyed by surprise, or even occupied—and it would be pleasanter than hell. Beelzebub cunningly prepares the way for Satan by suggesting that a reconnaissance should be undertaken to test the validity of his plan. This is accepted with enthusiasm.

NOTES AND GLOSSARY:

front:	forehead (Latin: *frons*)
Atlantean:	like those of Atlas the Titan who, as punishment for his part in the war against Zeus—for the Titans also fought a war against the Olympian gods, the Titanomachia—was made to carry the heavens upon his shoulders
audience:	listening
these titles:	Thrones, Powers and Virtues were three of the orders of heavenly beings
style:	title
for so:	judging by the applause after Mammon's speech
doubtless:	very likely; heavily sarcastic
those:	the loyal angels, ruled by God's golden sceptre and not his rod of iron
What:	why

projecting:	planning
determined:	a Miltonic play upon words; one meaning is 'terminated, put an end to us', the other 'decided'—while we propose, God disposes
Vouchsafed or sought	offered by God or requested by us
to our power:	to the limit of our power
reluctance:	resistance
occasion want:	opportunity be lacking
fame:	rumour (Latin: *fama*) as in I.651
To their defence:	to be defended by man alone. Beelzebub cleverly placates Moloch by applying his proposal of attack to earth, not heaven
repenting:	that He had ever created them to replace us
disturbance:	distress
frail original:	feeble founder of their race, Adam
Advise:	consider
Hatching:	creating, but only like a bird sitting on an egg. Milton's choice of vocabulary frequently indicates the speaker's precise tone of voice—here scornful. See also line 242 above
confound:	ruin
one root:	Adam
states:	estates, parliament

Book II, lines 290–520

Congratulating his followers on the wisdom of their decision, Satan calls for a volunteer to undertake the hazardous mission of reconnoitring earth. None being forthcoming—as Satan had anticipated—he offers to go himself to observe and to take any appropriate action possible; thus he confirms his right to command. He instructs them, while he is away, to follow that part of Mammon's plan which involves making the most of hell's resources and amenities. Having achieved his purpose, Satan brings the council to a swift conclusion.

NOTES AND GLOSSARY:

Synod:	usually an ecclesiastical gathering, but can also be used of planets (see X.661)
like to what:	you are great, and so are your decisions
confines:	frontiers of heaven
tempt:	try, test
palpable obscure:	darkness that can be felt. Milton gives a sense of vastness by his use of an abstract adjective in place of a noun

uncouth:	unmapped, hitherto unknown
indefatigable:	incapable of fatigue
vast abrupt:	the huge gap between hell and the universe, that is, Chaos. Again Milton uses an adjective for a noun
arrive:	arrive at, reach
stations:	guards (Latin: *stationes*)
lines 414–15:	The infernal spy will have to exercise great care; so must they in choosing him
suffrage:	vote
suspense:	attentive, waiting for the result
Astonished:	dismayed at the prospect
prime:	senior members
proffer:	volunteer
transcendent:	surpassing; worthy to be leader, even though in evil
demur:	non-acceptance; no one had actually objected
convex:	vault
unessential:	having no substance
abortive gulf:	the traveller through Chaos may never survive to emerge, like an aborted foetus
moment:	importance
Wherefore:	a question—'why?'—if the punctuation of the fourth (1688) and subsequent editions is followed; a statement—'for this reason'—if the earlier omission of the question-mark in line 456 is accepted
intend:	consider
respite:	give temporary relief
deceive:	persuade yourselves that things are better than they really are
coasts:	regions
prevented:	forestalled; a good example of a word used with its Latin meaning (*prævenire*). Satan does not want anyone else to gain cheap credit by belatedly volunteering; but they fear him as much as the mission
awful:	full of awe
lines 483:	A virtue like loyalty may be inspired by an evil leader or an unworthy cause and is not to be compared in value to spiritual virtues. Nor can salvation be achieved through good works, Milton believed, but by divine grace (see the Bible, Ephesians 2.8–9: 'by grace are ye saved … not of works'). And many outward virtues are inspired by secret ambition or a lust for glory, unworthy motives

doubtful consultations dark: Milton often places an adjective on either side of the noun they qualify

element:	sky
If chance:	if it should happen that
levy:	wage (by means of levied troops)
enow:	enough, sufficient
Stygian:	of the river Styx, in hell; thus also, of hell
paramount:	chief
globe:	on all sides and above, enclosing him in a globe
emblazonry:	shields emblazoned with heraldic devices
horrent:	bristling
bid cry:	ordered to be proclaimed
alchemy:	brass alloy with the appearance of gold; symbolic of hell's valueless imitation of heaven

---

Book II, lines 521–628

The various occupations of the fallen angels described: athletic contests; music and philosophical discussions; exploration to the limits of their new domain.

NOTES AND GLOSSARY:

ranged:	drawn up in ranks
several:	separate
entertain:	pass, while away
sublime:	uplifted
line 530:	Games were held in classical Greece at Olympia and Delphi in honour of Apollo, the Pythian god. Heroic games are also part of the epic tradition
shun the goal:	narrowly avoid the turning-post in a chariot race
fronted brigads:	opposing teams in a tournament
lines 533–538:	Graphic picture of cloud-formations driven by storm-winds. An epic simile
van:	vanguard
Prick:	ride; a chivalric term. Single wisps stream out in front of the banks of heavy storm-clouds
welkin:	sky
Typhoean:	Typhoeus (Typhon, I.199) hurled mountains against Zeus in the Giants' War; probably selected here because his name means 'whirlwind'
fell:	destructive
lines 542–6:	Hercules, grandson of Alcæus, returning from Œchalia sent his young companion Lichas ahead to fetch a new white robe in which he could offer

sacrifice to Zeus. Deianira, his wife, had been told by the dying Nestor, a centaur who had been killed by Hercules' poisoned arrow while trying to abduct her, to dip a robe in his blood and to send it to Hercules if she ever had cause to doubt his fidelity. This robe she sent with Lichas, not realising how deadly it was. Unable to tear the robe off and mad with pain, Hercules hurled Lichas into the Euboic Sea (the Aegean north-east of Athens), climbed mount Œta in Thessaly and ripped up pine trees to make a pyre on which he burned himself to death. (See Ovid, *Metamorphoses*, IX)

Retreated:	withdrawn, secluded
virtue:	strength. The fallen angels present the usual excuses for their fall, this time in song
partial:	prejudiced—in favour of themselves
Suspended:	held rapt
took:	enchanted
lines 557–561:	Even the fallen angels cannot resolve the eternal bitter controversy between free will and predestination
apathy:	freedom from the passion with which it is contrasted; a Stoic doctrine. Milton is here attacking the validity of scholastic disputation and Greek philosophical argument. He himself had been taught by this method of arguing the relative merits of philosophical opposites. (See E.M.W. Tillyard, *The Miltonic Setting*, Chatto and Windus, London, 1957, p.15)
obdured:	made hard
gross:	compact
Lethe:	This river is separated from the other four. The spirits of human dead, drinking its waters, forget their life on earth; but the rebel angels are not to be permitted such comfortable oblivion
labyrinth:	with many twisting channels
flood:	river
line 590:	The hail, piled up in heaps by the wind, gives the appearance of ruined buildings
Serbonian bog:	a dried-up lake in the Nile delta between Damietta and a large sand-dune called Mount Casius. Sometimes it fills up with sand, and a Persian army once marched into it and sank
frore:	freezing. Extreme cold imparts a burning sensation

Furies:	minor goddesses, instruments of divine vengeance. Harpies were female monsters with wings and hooked talons instead of feet
haled:	dragged
revolutions:	times, seasons
starve:	perish, not merely of hunger (Old English: *steorfan*, to die)
sound:	strait, estuary
withstands:	forbids, prevents
Medusa:	in Greek legend, the chief of three female monsters called Gorgons, with snakes instead of hair on their heads, so ugly that they turned all who looked on them to stone. Beheaded by Perseus
Tantalus:	In Greek legend, he was punished by Zeus by being placed in a lake with fruit growing over his head. Whenever he bent to drink, the waters receded, and the fruit when he ate it turned to ashes in his mouth; hence the word 'tantalise'
forlorn:	hopeless and lost
adventurous bands:	bands of exploring angels
for evil only good:	evil is the only good that this lost world knows
prodigious:	unnatural
Hydra ... Chimæras:	the Lernean Hydra was a monster with nine heads; every time Hercules cut one off, two grew in its place, so he strangled it with his bare hands. A Chimæra was a three-headed, fire-breathing monster, part lion, part dragon, part goat. These monsters stand for the worst that human imagination can conjure up

---

Book II, lines 629–1055

Satan sets off on his mission. Reaching the ninefold gates of hell, he encounters their twin guardians, Sin and Death. Sin prevents a battle between Satan and Death by revealing that Death is Satan's son by her, his daughter, incestuously conceived during the war in heaven. They agree that Sin shall unlock hell's gates and let Satan out; in return, Sin and Death shall range at will in the new world of man should Satan's mission prove successful. They begin to build a causeway to link hell with earth as Satan flies on through the realm of Chaos and old Night unopposed; unopposed because Chaos is angry that God has twice recently taken territory from him—once to create hell and once to create the new world. Reaching the outer limits of the universe and flying close enough to heaven to see its glittering ramparts in the distance, Satan alights at the point of entry into the planetary system, the spot where the golden chain joining the universe to heaven penetrates its outer surface.

NOTES AND GLOSSARY:

Adversary: the word 'Satan' means adversary
design: ambition
Explores: puts to the proof
concave: roof, vault
lines 636–42: In this epic simile, Satan is compared to a fleet of East Indiamen, armed merchant vessels, sailing from Bengal or two of the Spice Islands (the Moluccas), close-hauled to the trade winds across the Indian Ocean, south towards the Cape of Good Hope. Their sailing by night presents no problem, since Satan is visible in the darkness of hell; but if 'Hangs in the clouds' means that they appear from a distance to be in the clouds because of a mirage, it must be by day. 'Ply' can be rendered 'make their way', or in the specialised sense of 'work to windward'; 'stemming is 'pressing their stems (bows) forward', breasting the waves
impaled: enclosed
fold: coil
Voluminous: rolled up like a scroll (Latin: *volumen*)
mortal: deadly
cry: pack
line 655: Cerberus was the three-headed dog that guarded the gates of Hades
list: chose
lines 659–61: Sin's dogs are more to be abhorred than those which grew from Scylla's womb when she bathed in a pool bewitched by envious Circe; she was subsequently changed into a dangerous rock situated between Sicily and Calabria, the most southerly province of Italy. An epic comparison
Vexed: plagued
hoarse: from the sound of the sea beating on the shore
night-hag: Hecate, the Greek goddess of witchcraft and portress of Hades; she helped Circe to bewitch Scylla. She is followed by a pack of hellhounds
called: summoned by her worshippers
line 664: Witches were supposed to specialise in infanticide
Lapland: the traditional home of witchcraft and the centre of the cult of Hecate

labouring:	The moon was supposed to be affected by witchcraft; here she is driven into eclipse (see I.597) by the witches' spells (*charms*)
dart:	javelin
admired:	wondered
folly:	results of your foolhardiness
goblin:	evil spirit
third part:	based on the allegorical interpretation of the Bible, Revelation 12.4, where the dragon's tail is said to have drawn after him the third part of the stars of heaven. Satan himself claims that nearly half the heavenly host was on his side, but the accepted proportion is one-tenth of the angels
Conjured:	usually rendered 'sworn together in brotherhood' (Latin: *coniurati*); but 'bewitched into conspiring' gives better sense
line 696:	'Do you count yourself among the spirits of heaven?' Death replies to Satan's taunt in line 687, and neatly caps 'Hell-born' with 'Hell-doomed'
lines 708–711:	Ophiucus, 'the Serpent-bearer', was a constellation in the northern ('artic') sky. Comets were supposed to presage misfortune, and one that the diarist John Evelyn (1620–1706) records as appearing in 1618 was believed to have caused the Thirty Years' War
horrid hair:	the comet's tail is both bristling in its appearance and terrible in its threat of disaster
heaven's artillery:	thunder and lightning
Caspian:	a notoriously stormy sea
mid air:	the middle of the three regions of air and the one in which storms were supposedly created (see note on 'the middle air', p.28)
like:	likely. Christ will ultimately overcome both Satan and Death
bend:	aim
pest:	plague; a word with a much more serious connotation in the time of the Great Plague of London (1665) than nowadays
these:	these words
Prevented:	delayed (see note on 'prevented', p.39)
first met:	when first we met
lines 755–5:	Although the obvious comparison is with Eve's creation out of Adam's left side, a closer analogy is with the goddess Athene springing full-grown from the head of Zeus

Portentous:	full of evil portent
thy perfect image:	as the Son is of the Father
fields:	battles
pitch:	height
nether shape:	from the waist down Sin changed into snakes
line 787:	Sin cried out 'Death!' because she thought he was going to kill her, not because she recognised who he was
conscious terrors:	fears bred of knowledge of guilt. Sin's offspring vex her conscience as well as her body
in opposition:	on the other side of the gateway; a term used in astrology to describe two planets in opposite signs of the zodiac
bane:	slayer (Old English: *bana*)
line 809:	Sin also recognises Fate as the supreme power
heavenly:	in heaven
mortal dint:	fatal stroke
Save he:	except God
lore:	lesson
pledge of dalliance:	visible token of our love-making
pretences:	claims
uncouth:	bottomless
concurring signs:	Satan does not reveal that these corroboratory indications are of a new world having been created
purlieus:	outskirts
our vacant room:	the gap left by the eviction of the rebel angels; but they have not been placed in heaven itself, for fear of renewed rebellion in the future
more removed:	farther away
surcharged:	overfilled
potent:	powerful
hap to move new broils:	chance to set new disturbances in train
be this:	whether it is this or some more secret purpose
buxom:	yielding (Old English: *bugan*, to bend). At a medieval marriage the bride promised to obey her husband and be 'buxom and blithe in bed and at board'
embalmed:	made fragrant. Their new domain will be much pleasanter than their present habitation
famine:	hunger
maw:	stomach (of an animal)
Destined to:	dedicated to
bespake:	addressed
by due:	by right

office: duty

voluptuous: dedicated to an existence of everlasting sensual pleasure. She will stand at her father's right hand as the Son does at God's

rolling: she cannot walk

but: except for

intricate wards: the cunningly-cut incisions in the key matching the notches inside the lock

Erebus: hell itself, or possibly its forecourt

redounding: surging outwards in clouds

hoary: grey with age

ancestors of Nature: predecessors of the created universe, which had been carved out of their anarchic realm by God

by confusion stand: remain supreme because of the divisions of others

four champions: according to medieval medical theory, the four elements of which the universe is composed are repeated in four humours which are present in man's body: earth is cold and dry, and so is melancholy; air is hot and moist, and so is blood ('sanguis'); water is cold and moist, and so is phlegm; fire is hot and dry, and so is choler. When in good health, a man keeps these four humours in balance; but the preponderance of any one humour will impair that health and the doctor must take steps, based on the patient's symptoms, to restore the balance

maistrie: mastery, domination. Milton uses the terminology of chivalry to describe the struggle among the elements

embryon atoms: the atoms which in the universe will belong to one or other of the four elements are embryonic here in Chaos, and have not yet decided where to settle; whichever element they favour temporarily gains the upper hand by weight of numbers

Barca or Cyrene: in Libya, hence 'torrid'

Levied: a Miltonic play upon words: it means 'lifted up' and also 'enlisted'

poise: add weight to. A secondary meaning of the verb: the winds gain strength from the weight of the grains of sand they whip up, and become sandstorms

more embroils: complicates further

line 911: The universe was formed out of chaos and may eventually return to it

pregnant causes: embryonic matter; potentially belonging to one of the four elements. According to Aristotle, everything had four causes: what it is made of—the material cause (line 916); what produces it—the efficient cause; what gives it its form—the formal cause; and what it is for—the final cause

them ordain: should appoint them to become the materials from which new worlds are to be made

frith: estuary, firth

pealed: made to resound

Bellona: Roman goddess of war

frame of heaven: fabric of the sky

axle: the poles around which the earth rotates

steadfast: in the Ptolemaic system, the earth was its stationary centre

vans: wings (Italian: *vanni*)

line 930: Shot upwards in a cloud of smoke, Satan hits an air-pocket and plummets downward

pennons: pinions, wings (Latin: *pennae*)

rebuff: counterthrust

Instinct: charged

nitre: saltpetre. Satan is blown upwards by the natural gunpowder of a thundercloud

Syrtis: quicksand near Tripoli

nigh foundered: half sinking

crude consistence: mixture of sea and land

behoves him: he needs, would be glad of

gryphon: griffin, a mixture of eagle and lion: popular as a heraldic device. An epic simile

moory: marshy

Arimaspian: the Arimaspi ('one-eyed'), a tribe against whom the gryphon was supposed to guard the gold from the Siberian mines

straight, rough, dense, or rare: level or uneven ground, thick or thin matter

plies: makes his way

nearest coast: the nearest way to a point where the darkness borders on light

straight: suddenly

pavilion: palace

wasteful: desolate

sable-vested: clad in black

Orcus: Dis or Pluto, god of Hades ('Ades')

name of Demogorgon: Demogorgon himself; a Latin construction. Demogorgon was a mysterious deity, all the more powerful for remaining undefined in the background of a rather anthropomorphic hierarchy of classical gods. Edmund Spenser (1552?–99) in *Faerie Queene*, IV.2.47, makes him lord of chaos

various: different—each telling a contradictory story. These are allegorical personifications

Confine with: border on

profound: adjective used as a noun

behoof: advantage. If correctly directed, Satan will repay Chaos by restoring the new universe to his dominions

anarch old: Chaos, ancient lord of anarchy

ruin: fall

lines 999–1000: 'If all I can do will help defend what little is left to me'. The syntax in chaos is as confused as everything else!

intestine broils: civil wars

pyramid of fire: an appropriate image. Satan rises like a rocket, leaving an expanding trail of flame behind him

lines 1016–20: Satan's journey is more difficult than that of Jason and the Argonauts between the clashing rocks of the Bosphorus, or that of Ulysses between the rock of Scylla (II.660) and the whirlpool Charybdis in the straits of Messina. An epic comparison

larboard: port side, the left side

amain: with all speed

utmost orb: outermost sphere of the Ptolemaic system

sacred influence: the actual light of the sun

nature: the created universe. The limits of Chaos' jurisdiction

dubious: still faint

holds: steers towards

emptier: than chaos had been

Weighs: rests on

undetermined: too extensive for him to determine whether it was square or round

living: living, uncut. In Revelation 21.19 one of the foundations of heaven is sapphire

in bigness as a star: To Satan on the outer edge of the universe, the earth would appear minute

Thither: Satan's easiest point of entry into the universe is where the chain joins it to heaven

Part 3

Commentary

IT HAS ALREADY been pointed out (p.15) that the story of *Paradise Lost* does not begin at the beginning, go on to the end, and then stop; it begins in the middle, goes back to the beginning, reaches its climax in the fall and finally looks forward into the future. Nor is each book concerned with the same themes, though each contributes to the whole—the demonstration of how mankind came to be created, to be tempted, to sin and to be promised redemption: for example, Book III is primarily concerned with the problem of free will; Books V and VI with the war in heaven; Book VII with the creation; Book VIII with the discoveries of Galileo; and Book IX with man's fall. Books I and II raise a number of matters of interest—some shared with other Books and some peculiar to themselves—which must now be examined, discussed and understood.

Cosmology

The details of Milton's cosmological scheme have already been set forth in the Introduction (pp.10–11), but Books I and II concentrate on certain aspects of it. The beauties of the heaven they have lost are frequently spoken of by the fallen angels as a contrast to the horrors of the hell they now endure:

> Is this the region, this the soil, the clime,
> Said then the lost archangel, this the seat
> That we must change for heaven, this mournful gloom
> For that celestial light? Be it so, since he
> Who now is sovereign can dispose and bid
> What shall be right: furthest from him is best
> Whom reason hath equalled, force hath made supreme
> Above his equals. Farewell happy fields
> Where joy for ever dwells: hail horrors, hail
> Infernal world, and thou profoundest hell
> Receive thy new possessor.
>
> (I.242–52)

Hell itself is graphically described: its burning lake (I.222–37); its buried treasure (I.670–709); its remoter regions (II.570–628); its ninefold walls of adamant and its gates guarded by the grim monsters, Sin and Death (II.643–73). Outside lies the realm of Chaos and Old Night and, as Satan wings his way towards the newly-created universe with the object of seducing man from God's service, Sin and Death begin to build their fatal causeway behind him (II.1024–30). Book II ends as Satan reaches the point on the outer surface of the universe where it hangs suspended from heaven by a golden chain. This gap provides him with a means of entry (II.1051–2).

The backdrop of Milton's cosmos, against which the action of *Paradise Lost* takes place, is vast; and this sense of vastness is increased by Milton's deliberate use of large numbers of abstract adjectives, some of them taking the place of nouns. In Book II, the immense void between hell's gates and the newly-created universe—well named by Satan 'this profound' in line 980—is twice described in this manner:

> Who shall tempt with wandering feet
> The dark unbottomed infinite abyss
> And through the palpable obscure find out
> His uncouth way, or spread his airy flight
> Upborne with indefatigable wings
> Over the vast abrupt, ere he arrive
> The happy isle.
>
> (II.404–10)

and again:

> ... with lonely steps to treat
> The unfounded deep, and through the void immense
> To search with wandering quest a place foretold
>
> (II.828–30)

And yet, for all its vastness, Milton's cosmos remains ordered and controlled; for this, Milton's adoption of the clearly delineated Ptolemaic system of astronomy, in preference to the open-ended Copernican system which Book VII proves he knew to be scientifically correct, must be held to be largely responsible.

Theology

The first two books of *Paradise Lost* are not concerned with any major theological controversy, like the exact nature of the Son or whether our world was created out of nothing or was a part of God Himself. The following points, however, are worthy of mention.

Fallen angels and pagan gods

Milton adopts the view that the fallen angels lost their original names after their fall, and became known to man as the heathen idols of the Old

Testament and the pagan deities of Egypt, Greece and Rome:

> Then were they known to men by various names,
> And various idols through the heathen world. (I.374–5)

The long list that extends from I.356 to 521 shows both the extent of
Milton's learning and the dual nature of his cultural debt to the
scriptures and the Classics. Details of those fallen angels who have
become heathen deities will be found in the explanatory notes in Part 2,
pp.23–4

Holy spirit and heavenly Muse

Readers of Books I and II, and particularly of the opening lines, might
be left in some uncertainty as to the exact nature of the Spirit Milton is
here invoking. Is it the Holy Ghost, that rather nebulous third person of
the Trinity? It would certainly seem so from lines 17–22. And yet in
Book VII.1–39 Milton makes it abundantly clear that he is invoking
Urania, actually addressing her twice by name; but Urania was the Muse
of astronomy, not of epic poetry, and Milton states plainly that it is only
the name that is the same:

> Descend from heaven Urania, by that name
> If rightly thou art called, whose voice divine
> Following, above the Olympian hill I soar,
> Above the flight of Pegasean wing.
> The meaning, not the name I call: for thou
> Nor of the Muses nine, nor on the top
> Of old Olympus dwell'st, but heavenly born,
> Before the hills appeared, or fountain flowed,
> Thou with eternal Wisdom didst converse,
> Wisdom thy sister, and with her didst play
> In presence of the almighty Father, pleased
> With thy celestial song. (VII.1–12)

If we accept that Urania was the name Milton gave to his Muse of
Christian epic, there is no contradiction: Milton recognises the power
and pre-eminence of the Holy Spirit from a religious point of view, and
certainly asks for help and instruction from this source in I.17–22; but,
as an artist, he was writing an epic, and epic poets began by invoking a
Muse. Milton therefore also begins by invoking a Muse, but, insisting
on the artistic as well as the moral superiority of the scriptural over
the classical (see also Bohn, Vol. 2, pp.478–9) and *Paradise Regained*,
IV.330–50), he places his Muse on Moses's mountain rather than
Parnassus. He certainly regarded himself as divinely inspired, and would
lie in bed in the early morning until he had composed a passage in his

head, when he would call out that he was 'ready to be milked'. He was always deeply interested in his own creative process as a poet, and the openings of Books III, VII and particularly IX repeat the concern with poetic composition shown in Book I and, earlier, in 'Lycidas' and the 'Twenty-Third Birthday' sonnet.

Free will

One of the most vexed of theological questions has always been the extent to which a man—or a fallen angel—is free to choose his own course of action. Milton's own position here is very clear, and his repeated insistence that man's power of reason gives him the freedom to choose between good and evil brought him into conflict with the Presbyterian faction of the Republican party with its Calvinistic insistence on predestination and the election of the chosen few (themselves) to everlasting bliss. In a speech in Book III.95–128, God the Father makes it clear that man was created strong enough to have resisted temptation, but left free to fall; and the fact that God foreknew that he would fall did not of itself bring the fall about. The fallen angels also are at pains to stress their independence. They were free to choose their own path, and Satan claims their leadership not only by heavenly decree but by his own merit, pre-eminence in battle and by free election. How then do the angels account for their defeat, if their cause was just and their power equal to God's? They frequently suggest that Chance, not God, has been the cause of their fall. In chaos, 'Chance governs all' (II.910). They also doubt whether the divine essence of which they are made *can* be destroyed, even by God; Moloch proposes a renewal of the battle on the grounds that, if they can be annihilated, they will at least be at peace in oblivion, whereas if they cannot be destroyed, their condition cannot be changed for the worse. Sin warns her father, Satan, that not even he is proof against Death's dart (II.810–14). But we are left in some uncertainty as to the exact composition of the fallen angels—the nature of their divine essence and ethereal temper—though the orthodox explanation of the remarkable degree of freedom enjoyed by the devils is that it is by God's permission and is all part of this grand design for the World, much of which is beyond mere human understanding.

Epic and the epic hero

The place of *Paradise Lost* in the history of epic poetry has already been discussed in Part 1 (pp.11–13). Its unique quality is that it transcends the nationalistic subjects of Renaissance epic and deals with the universal topic of the fall of man. But in many other respects Milton consciously follows the epic pattern. Not merely are supernatural characters introduced: *all* the characters in Books I and II are superhuman. The Muse's aid is invoked, since human endeavour alone cannot support so weighty a subject; the weapons of the heroes are described (Satan's shield and spear, I.284–96); and some of the fallen angels pass the time while Satan is away on reconnaissance by indulging in heroic games and chariot races (II.528–38).

Epic similes

Epic similes abound in these first two books. The epic or Homeric simile is much longer than an ordinary poetic comparison; it is a complete picture in itself, a vignette—so called from the illustrations included in the margins of manuscripts and enclosed within the tendrils of entwining vines. Such similes, while not directly furthering the narrative, enlarge the reader's knowledge of the situation by analogy. In *Paradise Lost*, the epic similes serve a special purpose by bringing the superhuman subject within the compass of human experience; Milton uses his vast learning to show his readers what it was like to live in a world they could never know, and the measure of his success is that most Englishmen would describe hell and the fall in Miltonic terms—the Book of Genesis in the Bible makes no mention of any Satan in the Garden of Eden; only the serpent is there.

These epic similes merit detailed study. The first (I.196–209) compares Satan in size to the mighty monsters of nature and of myth. And immediately we come upon one of the principal barriers to the modern appreciation of Milton: it does not help us to know that Satan was as huge as Briareus or Typhon when our lack of classical—and in other cases biblical—learning prevents us from knowing who these monsters were. But this Milton could not have foreseen, any more than he could foresee that his universal topic of the fall of man was a subject that future generations would indeed be willing to let die. Other epic similes fall into the same category of the obscure—for example the volcanoes of Latin literature in I.230–7; less so the better-known story of Pharaoh and the plagues of Egypt (I.338–44); less still the comparison of Satan's shield to the moon seen through Galileo's telescope and his spear to the mast of some great Norwegian ship (I. 284–96). Nature similes we can comprehend, as when the fallen Satan is compared to the sun in eclipse (I.589–99); when the monsters are fabulous, like the gryphon in II.943, we are less enlightened; and to most of us the long lists of vast armies from classics and romances (I.573–88) mean very little. This last example is worth quoting in full, not merely because the principal sources of Milton's extensive learning are again in evidence, but because it illustrates his method of stressing the epic quality of his subject by claiming that the most celebrated examples of a certain characteristic—

in this case numerousness—cannot equal what he is writing about:

> ... for never since created man,
> Met such embodied force, as named with these
> Could merit more than that small infantry
> Warred on by cranes: though all the Giant brood
> Of Phlegra with the heroic race were joined
> That fought at Thebes and Ilium, on each side
> Mixed with auxiliar gods; and what resounds
> In fable or romance of Uther's son
> Begirt with British and Armoric knights;
> And all who since, baptized or infidel
> Jousted in Aspramont or Montalban,
> Damasco, or Marocco, or Trebisond,
> Or whom Biserta sent from Afric shore
> When Charlemain with all his peerage fell
> By Fontarabbia. Thus far these beyond
> Compare of mortal prowess.
>
> (I.573–588)

The epic hero

The character of the hero in every epic gives us some notion of the ideals of the age and the society that gave the epic birth. In the Homeric period, personal glory won on the field of battle was the aim of every warrior, and in heroic epic the heroes strive for a reputation for military prowess: Achilles chooses a short life and a brilliant one in preference to a long and undistinguished career, while Beowulf is rewarded for slaying Grendel not merely with rich gifts but by being assured that by this deed he has made certain that his renown will live for ever. It is remarkable that, in the *Iliad*, Achilles behaves like a spoilt child, skulking in his tent while his comrades are defeated, because he thinks he has been robbed of a slave girl; Hector on the other hand is a loving husband and father, leading the Trojans in a defensive war he never sought but which was thrust upon him by his brother's folly. Yet when Achilles and Hector meet, it is Achilles who triumphs; Hector may have the nobler character, but Achilles has the swifter foot and the surer eye, the greater will to power and lust for glory.

With the advent of Virgil and the secondary epic, the character of the hero changed. Virgil wrote the *Aeneid* as a compliment to the new emperor, Augustus; his hero, Aeneas, is an empire builder, destined to found Rome. But he is no mere seeker of glory. He prefers to make treaties and, when fight he must, he fights single combats to prevent wholesale slaughter. And he reflects the philosophical tendencies of his creator's age by proving that, before he is fit to found an empire, he is capable of gaining control over himself and rising above such distractions and disasters as the love of Dido and the destruction of his fleet. If there is a hero in the old Homeric pattern in the *Aeneid* it is Turnus, the defeated suitor for Lavinia's hand, not Aeneas. This point, that an old-time hero can, because of the changing fashions of an age, become a new-style villain, was not lost on Milton.

The significance of this process to an understanding of Milton becomes apparent if we look closely at his own comment in Book IX. He claims that to tell the story of man's fall is a

> ... sad task, yet argument
> Not less but more heroic than the wrath
> Of stern Achilles on his foe pursued
> Thrice fugitive about Troy wall; or rage
> Of Turnus for Lavinia disespoused.
>
> (IX.13–17)

Two points should be noticed: that what constitutes the heroic is subject to change, and has changed from the mere pursuit of military glory and martial reputation; and that the Virgilian character who represents to Milton what needs to be superseded is Turnus, not Aeneas. What then is the Miltonic idea of a hero? He tells us often enough, but most clearly in *Areopagitica*:

> I cannot praise a fugitive and cloistered virtue unexercised and unbreathed, that never sallies out and seeks her adversary, but slinks out of the race, where that immortal garland is to be run for, not without dust and heat. Assuredly we bring not innocence into the world, we bring impurity much rather; that which purifies us is trial, and trial is by what is contrary. That virtue therefore which is but a youngling in the contemplation of evil, and knows not the utmost that vice promises to her followers, and rejects it, is but a blank virtue, not a pure; her whiteness is but an excremental whiteness; which was the reason why our sage and serious poet Spenser, (whom I dare be known to think a better teacher than Scotus or Aquinas,) describing true temperance under the person of Guion, brings him in with his palmer through the cave of Mammon, and the bower of earthly bliss, that he might see and know, and yet abstain. (Bohn, Vol. 2, p.68)

The Miltonic hero, then, is still a warrior, winning his victories over intemperance on the battlefields of the spirit: in him we can see the Platonic rational soul overcoming the soul irrational through lust and the soul irrational through anger; and also the true warfaring Puritan who, aided by divine grace, goes out to face sin and temptation and push back the forces of darkness and evil.

Satan

The question of whether Satan is the hero of *Paradise Lost* presents no problem if we understand our Miltonic hero. Satan has fallen through intemperance. He has committed incest with his daughter, Sin (II.762–76). He has reached beyond the bounds of moderation in his pride, ambition, envy and rage. And he succeeds in seducing Adam and Eve into intemperance.

Why then has Milton been claimed to be of the Devil's party, even if without knowing it? First, because the word 'hero' has two meanings in English: it indicates the central figure in a work of art—and that Satan certainly is in *Paradise Lost*, I and II; and it indicates the character with whom the reader most readily identifies or at least sympathises—and though in many cases the two are the same character, this is not so in *Paradise Lost*. A second reason is that, on the evidence of great poetry alone, Milton is at his most memorable in the early books of *Paradise Lost*, at the very time when Satan holds the centre of the stage. And let us make no mistake: Satan possesses many admirable characteristics—courage, leadership, a willingness to undertake what no one else dares to do, the imagination to realise his enemy's weakness and the initiative to exploit it. He has fought and lost, and now he is going to continue the fight by other means; and we cannot but admire his courage and wholeheartedness, even though his purpose is utterly evil. This is called antinomism—working towards an evil end in a manner worthy of a good one. And the evidence of the text certainly points to Milton's consciousness of Satan's potential worth:

Pre-eminence: concern for his followers
   ... he above the rest
In shape and gesture proudly eminent
Stood like a tower; his form had yet not lost
All her original brightness, nor appeared
Less than archangel ruined, and the excess
Of glory obscured. (I.589–94)

      Darkened so, yet shone
Above them all the archangel: but his face
Deep scars of thunder had intrenched, and care
Sat on his faded cheek, but under brows
Of dauntless courage, and considerate pride
Waiting revenge; cruel his eye, but cast
Signs of remorse and passion to behold
The fellows of his crime, the followers rather
(Far other once beheld in bliss) condemned
For ever now to have their lot in pain. (I.599–608)

Defiant in defeat
>   What though the field be lost?
> All is not lost; the unconquerable will,
> And study of revenge, immortal hate,
> And courage never to submit or yield:
> And what is else not to be overcome?
> That glory never shall his wrath or might
> Extort from me. To bow and sue for grace
> With suppliant knee, and deify his power,
> Who from the terror of this arm so late
> Doubted his empire, that were low indeed,
> That were an ignominy and shame beneath
> This downfall. (I.105–116)

Antinomism: courage
> So farewell hope, and with hope farewell fear,
> Farewell remorse: all good to me is lost;
> Evil be thou my good. (IV.108–10)

Why did Milton give Satan so outstanding a character? To make his ultimate degeneration into a snake, with his triumph turning to ashes in his mouth all the more remarkable? Perhaps, to some extent. But it seems that Milton sought to follow Virgil, or even go one step farther. Satan, like Turnus, is intended to be an old-style hero; indeed Henry Bradley, in an essay entitled 'The Caedmonian Genesis',* suggests that Milton must have known the Old English poem, so similar are the speeches and traits of character of Satan in *Paradise Lost* and the Heroic fragment. But whereas Virgil was content to let his hero, Aeneas, reflect the imperial sentiments and stoic philosophy of his own age, Milton sought to prompt his age 'to quit their clogs' as he says in Sonnet XII, setting before them the Miltonic pattern of a hero, so superior in his temperance and his successful struggle against temptation to those warriors who merely won glory on the battlefield; this is quite clear from *Paradise Lost*, IX.5–45. Where Milton made his mistake was in believing that posterity was going to accept his view of what constitutes a hero; instead, it has obstinately continued to recognise the traditional heroic qualities manifested in Satan—qualities which Milton intended to be superseded, though he made a second mistake in not producing in *Paradise Lost* a convincing representative of his new pattern of hero. Satan is the character we remember, not just because he is the hero of *Paradise Lost*, but because he is the figure who possesses the most recognisably heroic characteristics.

---

*Essays and Studies of the English Association, No. 6, 1920.

Other characters

It seems convenient here to dispose briefly of the other characters in Books I and II. The main body of fallen angels who became heathen idols and classical gods are mere names; Sin, Death, Chaos and Old Night are personifications. The only personalities apart from Satan are the leading speakers at the infernal council. Chief of these is the final speaker, Satan's lieutenant and mouthpiece, and his companion on the burning lake in Book I, Beelzebub. The brief pen-portrait Milton draws of him shows his art of characterisation at its best, with an admirable balance between physical features and moral qualities:

> Which when Beelzebub perceived, than whom,
> Satan except, none higher sat, with grave
> Aspect he rose, and in his rising seemed
> A pillar of state; deep on his front engraven
> Deliberation sat and public care;
> And princely counsel in his face yet shone,
> Majestic though in ruin: sage he stood
> With Atlantean shoulders fit to bear
> The weight of mightiest monarchies; his look
> Drew audience and attention still as night
> Or summer's noontide air, while thus he spake. (II.299–309)

The other leading speakers in the great debate are inferior to Beelzebub as examples of characterisation because they are created to match the point of view they express rather than the reverse; normally, people express a point of view in keeping with their character. Moloch is blustering and aggressive, ranting away in support of a policy of victory or death. Belial of the pleasing manner and honeyed tongue recommends a policy of passivity in expectation of a commuted sentence. And Mammon, the most popular because he stands midway between dangerous defiance and spineless surrender, realistically proposes that they should make the best of things as they are and learn to live in the condition in which they now find themselves. Three speakers; three characters; three different reactions to the situation: a harangue on desperate revenge; a soothing eulogy of pacifism; and a plain recommendation to face facts and make the best of them.

Style

Varieties of poetic style

Paradise Lost is a literary or secondary epic, and one of the means by which the sublimity of primary epic was reproduced in secondary epic was in the conscious grandeur of the style. What has been called 'the sonorous orotund of Milton's organ-music' rolls out in majestic paragraphs of polysyllabic words of mainly classical origin; the first full stop in *Paradise Lost* does not appear until after a full sixteen lines. Other characteristics of the epic style have already been discussed, for example the epic simile; but the recent reference to the infernal debate in Book II indicated that, within the epic framework, there were other poetic styles. Milton shows not merely that he can argue in verse, but that he can argue logically, progressively and convincingly from more than one point of view and in more than one tone of voice. Moloch's speech is as abrupt as this description of him:

> He ceased/and next him Moloch/sceptred king/
> Stood up/the strongest and the fiercest spirit
> That fought in heaven/now fiercer by despair (II.43–5)

> My sentence is for open war/of wiles
> More unexpert/I boast not/them let those
> Contrive who need/or when they need/not now (II.51–3)

In contrast, Belial's tongue drops manna and he pleases the ear:

> And with persuasive accent thus began.
> I should be much for open war, O peers,
> As not behind in hate/if what was urged
> Main reason to persuade immediate war,
> Did not dissuade me most/and seem to cast
> Ominous conjecture on the whole success (II.119–123)

The words are longer and more Latinised, the speech-units are longer, and one part of the sentence runs on into another. Milton was, by virtue of his training in classical rhetoric and his activities as a pamphleteer, well schooled in debate and written argument, and this aspect of his genius, so apparent in Book II, is, because of changing fashions in educational method, largely lost upon his modern readers.

Paradise Lost, Books I and II, then, though predominantly epic, contain also the poetry of invocation and the poetry of polemic—both primarily rhetorical. Milton also shows mastery in narrative and descriptive poetry and in the occasional poetic pen-portraits of his characters.

Characteristics of style

The Homeric simile is an aspect of epic: it is also stylistic, a major characteristic of Milton's style in *Paradise Lost*. Similarly, many of the other features of epic we have been looking at could be included under the heading of style. But there is much in Milton's style that is not specifically or restrictively epic; these non-epic features of style, repeated elsewhere in Milton's other work, must now be examined.

Epic similes often contain other stylistic elements: biblical references or classical allusions; single-sentence paragraphs, because the vignette making up the epic simile is often one long sentence of complicated syntax and involved inter-relationship of its component parts; and proper names chosen partly for their literary, mythological, or historical associations, but also for their sound-value. Milton, a poet who was also a musician and whose awareness of sound was increased by his loss of sight, handled sounds with a fine discrimination that a modern spelling fails to show: 'sovran' (I.246), 'ammiral' (I.294), and 'haralds' (II.518) are derived from the Italian *sovrano, ammiraglia* and *araldo*, while 'highth' in I.24 and 282 is taken from Old English *hehthu* and is actually more etymologically correct than the normal 'height'. Personal pronouns have emphatic and unemphatic forms in Milton, indicated by the spelling in the original and reproduced in the Oxford edition—'mee' in II.18, for example. The choice of 'Fontarabbia' in preference to the more usual Roncesvalles, on the grounds of sound-value, rounds off one of Milton's most celebrated collections of proper names:

> and what resounds
> In fable or romance of Uther's son
> Begirt with British and Armoric knights;
> And all who since, baptized or infidel
> Jousted in Aspramont or Montalban,
> Damasco, or Marocco, or Trebisond,
> Or whom Biserta sent from Afric shore
> When Charlemain with all his peerage fell
> By Fontarabbia.   (I.579–587)

Similarly, a little-known Pharaoh is selected to stand for them all— because his name sounds right:

> he stood and called
> His legions, angel forms, who lay entranced
> Thick as autumnal leaves that strew the brooks
> In Vallambrosa, where the Etrurian shades
> Hight overarched imbower; or scattered sedge
> Afloat, when with fierce winds Orion armed
> Hath vexed the Red Sea coast, whose waves o'erthrew
> Busiris and his Memphian chivalry.   (I.300–7)

How mellifluous a proper name is Vallambrosa! Frequently, Milton arranges the order of sounds in proper names at the end of a paragraph to give a sense of finality in the enforced dropping of the voice—a falling cadence; 'Beneath Gibraltar to the Libyan sands' (I.355) is reminiscent of the well-known example in 'Lycidas' 63, 'Down the swift Hebrus to the Lesbian shore'.

From proper names and personal pronouns to adjectives. We have already seen adjectives used in place of nouns to give a sense of vastness—the 'palpable obscure' and 'vast abrupt' of II.406–9. Another adjectival characteristic of Miltonic verse is to increase the richness of meaning by placing an adjective on each side of the noun: 'uncouth errand sole' in II.827, or 'orient colours waving' in I.546.

But the most common usage involving adjectives is inversion, following the Latin rather than the English word order. Of the many examples, two from each Book will suffice: 'dungeon horrible' (I.61) and 'darkness visible' (I.63); 'void profound' (II.438) and 'mother bad' (II.849). Milton also borrows grammatical constructions from Latin—'what time' (I.36, from *quo tempore*); 'never since created man' (I.573); and 'Beelzebub . . . than whom, Satan except, none higher sat' (II.299–300); but his most remarkable Latin characteristic is his use of words in their Latin rather than their English sense—a habit confusing to the modern reader and too widely employed to illustrate by more than a list of the most striking examples:

Book I	46	ruin	*ruina*	falling
	167	if I fail not	*ni fallor*	if I am not mistaken
	312	abject	*abiectus*	thrown down
	320	virtue	*virtus*	strength
	563	horrid (II.513 horrent)	*horridus*	bristling
	651	fame (and II.346)	*fama*	rumour
	690	admire (and II.677)	*admiror*	wonder at
Book II	302	front	*frons*	forehead
	357	reluctance	*reluctans*	writhing in resistance
	467,739	prevented	*prævenire*	forestalled

Thus, although Milton himself insisted upon the superiority of form as well as of content of biblical over classical literature, and although on balance Old Testament references predominate in Book I, there is no doubt that the prevailing stylistic influence in *Paradise Lost* is Latin; if not of reference, certainly of vocabulary and of grammatical construction.

Part 4

Hints for study

Answering questions on the text

Three main types of written answer can be demanded: (a) the one written in your own time and with full reference to texts, works of criticism and biography, and all other aids; (b) the one written for an examination, in a limited time, but with reference to the text—but only the text—permitted; (c) the one written under strict examination conditions with a time limit and no external aids allowed. The reason for differentiating between (b) and (c) is the increasing tendency to reward sound critical judgement rather than the gift of a good memory.

Questions of type (a)

There is a mistaken idea in many educational institutions of what the aim of a literary examination is: it is *not* to give the candidates the opportunity to regurgitate all the information they have amassed about the writer and his works whose name appears in the question. So you should remember these points:

1. Select only that part of your knowledge or the material available to you which is strictly relevant to the question asked.

2. Read the actual text on the syllabus as often as you can and try and tell the examiner about its effect on you personally.

3. Although works of criticism by highly qualified specialists in the subject are valuable, they should be read to provoke thought and stimulate ideas only *after* you have read the text thoroughly and thought about it carefully.

4. Quotations should illustrate your point of view and strengthen your argument; but they must not become an end in themselves. An examiner will not relish—or reward—an essay that is three parts Milton and only one part candidate; he wants to know the candidate's views, which should be judiciously supported by quotations from and references to Milton's text.

Questions of types (b) and (c)

1. Know the text that has been set on the syllabus thoroughly before you go into the examination. Although a final reading through of the text is advisable, do not read works of criticism, sets of notes, or prepared answers just before the examination, for two reasons: what you have just read will be uppermost in your mind, and will unbalance the proportions of your material; secondly, if a question similar but not identical to one you have just been revising appears in the paper, you will tend to force the question to fit your prepared answer instead of writing an answer matched to the actual question. In both these cases, you will lose marks for irrelevance, the most common cause of failure in literary examinations.

2. After reading the question carefully, jot down the topics of major interest which it raises. These are going to become your paragraph headings; there should be at least three of them so that, with an introduction and a conclusion, you will have the optimum number of five paragraphs of average length—more if shorter, though fewer are rarely justified. Written answers should always conclude: never just stop; and each paragraph should deal with a different aspect of the question, though if you can run one paragraph smoothly into the next, so much the better.

3. Under your paragraph headings, jot down supporting references from the text; in (b) you will be able to note the line numbers from your text, but in (c) you will have to remember some word or phrase that will recall the required quotation or reference to mind when the time comes.

4. Take each paragraph-sheet separately and rearrange the subsidiary points into a coherent and progressive argument, moving your line-references out of strict chronological order to follow the ideas to which they belong.

5. From your new plan, write out your answer, adding a brief introductory paragraph and a conclusion. In (b), your line-references will now become quotations, in (c) they should be short quotations if you know them by heart, or references to show that you know the text. Remember that, if you do this, no examiner will penalise you, however much he may personally disagree with your interpretation. After all, what he is looking for is critical judgement and originality and independence of mind, not just the ability to sop up huge quantities of second- or third-hand material like a sponge, to be squeezed to order.

Type of question set on *Paradise Lost*, Books I and II

Let us apply these principles to *Paradise Lost*, Books I and II. The first essay in category (*a*) might be 'What topics does Milton cover in *Paradise Lost*, Books I and II?' The answer to this is contained in the sectional summaries, and the purpose of the question is to make the new student read the text thoroughly and familiarise himself with its content.

We can next proceed to questions on themes of content: first, those which can be covered from the text alone, such as 'Summarise the arguments advanced in the great debate in Pandæmonium in Book II, and say which you personally find most convincing'; secondly—and this after some instruction on the text has been given—themes which require some background knowledge, for instance, 'Illustrate from *Paradise Lost* I and II the steps taken by Milton to make his work an epic' (the material for this answer is to be found on pp.52–8. Next comes the type of question which necessitates the painstaking collection of material from the text—a test of your powers of application—its rearrangement and presentation as a unified and coherent written answer, for instance, 'Illustrate the principal characteristics of Milton's style in *Paradise Lost* I and II' (see pp.59–61). Finally, there is the type of question which demands a considerable amount of thought and originality from the individual student, plus a sound knowledge of the text on which he can draw to support his argument by quotation and reference; for instance, 'Is Satan in your view the hero of *Paradise Lost* I and II?' (This question is answered from a point of view no more and no less critically valid than a number of others, on pp.56–8).

Specimen question

It would be valuable to take one question not answered in the course of this study and to show how it might be tackled—a practical example of how to write an essay on Milton.

Compare Milton's use of biblical and classical materials in *Paradise Lost*, Books I and II.

To Milton and many of his contemporaries, using the Bible as a literary source was a matter of grave concern: could the divinely-inspired word of God be altered to the slightest extent in the interest of art? Milton decided that it could, although he considered the Bible, individually interpreted, to be of far greater authority than any organised Church. Certainly, he considered the Old Testament to be much superior to the literature of ancient Greece, not only in its content, but also in its form:

this he states clearly both in the *Reason of Church Government* (Bohn, Vol. 2, p.479) and in *Paradise Regained*, IV.331–50. In *Paradise Lost*, I and II, however, there is no direct conflict between these two major sources of literary inspiration, the biblical and the classical.

The Old Testament provides Milton with a considerable part of his narative material in Book I. He believed that the fallen angels lost the names they had borne in heaven before their fall and had taken the names of heathen idols, by which names they were worshipped by the tribes with whom the Hebrews came into contact, like the Ammonites, the Moabites and the Philistines. These gods parade in epic style in Book I.381–505, and two of the most important, the first and the last, Moloch and Belial, appear again as principal speakers in the great debate in Book II.

The Bible provides Milton with something more than narrative material; his illustrative material, the content of his epic similes and other comparisons, is often taken from the scriptures. For example, when he speaks of the vast numbers of fallen angels, he compares them to the army with which Pharaoh pursued the Israelites to the shores of the Red Sea (I.306–13), a passage which also illustrates Milton's relish for the sound-values of such proper names as Busiris and his Memphian chivalry.

The pagan gods of classical mythology are also identified with the fallen angels (I.506–21). The classics also provide the diversions for Satan's followers during his absence on his mission to earth—martial and athletic contests, music and debate, philosophy and exploration of the classical underworld (II.521–628). With this passage occurs a Homeric simile—itself a classical stylistic device—in which Milton's consciousness of sound-values is shown by his choice of the alternative form 'Alcides' for 'Hercules' or 'Herakles':

> As when Alcides from Œchalia crowned
> With conquest, felt the envenomed robe, and tore
> Through pain up by the roots Thessalian pines,
> And Lichas from the top of Œta threw
> Into the Euboic sea. (II.542–6)

Thus Milton uses his biblical and classical material for two identical purposes: the fallen angels become both the heathen idols of the Old Testament and the pagan deities of classical mythology; and the resounding proper names of Milton's epic similes are taken mainly from these two sources—when he wants size, he thinks of Leviathan or Briareus and Typhon, when quantity, Pharaoh's armies, the leaves of Vallambrosa, or the barbarian hordes invading the Roman Empire. Both sources, too, can be drawn on for discussion of themes less obvious than the principal ones: the New Testament for the nature of the Holy

Spirit whom Milton invokes in I.17; the colours of classical rhetoric for the variations in tone in the speeches of Book II, and the Latinised syntax and vocabulary of the whole work.

There are, however, some differences in Milton's use of his two main bodies of source material, slight though these are in comparison to the similarities. Milton was deeply learned in both, but whereas Old Testament material predominates in Book I in the much longer list of heathen idols and the greater number of scriptural illustrations, in Book II, where his narrative lacks scriptural authority, Milton relies almost exclusively on classical references even in his epic similes.

This must therefore be our conclusion. In Books I and II of *Paradise Lost*, Milton makes extensive and almost equal use of biblical and classical material; he possessed, and shows, a vast knowledge of both. Biblical and classical references reinforce or supplement each other in both narrative and illustration, and nowhere in this work is the conflict to be found between the two which unhappily occurs elsewhere, though Milton leaves us in no doubt that for him it is the Bible which has the advantage of being divinely inspired.

Part 5

Suggestions for further reading

The text

CAREY J., AND A. FOWLER, EDS.: *Milton*, Longmans Annotated English Poets Series, Longman, London, 1966. Full and erudite annotations and cross-references.

SUMNER, C.R., ED.: *Milton's Prose Works*, 5 vols., Bohn, London, 1848–53. Easier to handle than the Columbia Milton.

Milton's Complete Works, Columbia edition, 18 vols., University of Columbia Press, New York, 1931–8. The definitive edition.

Milton's Poetical Works, Oxford Standard Authors Series, Oxford University Press, London, 1904, revised 1969. Retains the original spelling important for Milton.

VERITY, A.W.: *Milton, 'Paradise Lost'*, 2 vols., Cambridge University Press, Cambridge, 1936. Good notes in Volume 2.

Biographies and criticism

DIEKHOFF J.S.: *Milton on Himself*, Cohen & West, London, 1966. Excellent collection of significant quotations from Milton's poetry and prose.

HANFORD, J.H.: *A Milton Handbook*, F.S. Crofts, New York, 1946. Essential to any thoughtful student of *Paradise Lost*.

SEWELL, W.A.: *A Study in Milton's Christian Doctrine*, Oxford University Press, London, 1939. Discusses Milton's theology.

TILLYARD, E.M.W.: *The Miltonic Setting*, Chatto & Windus, London, 1957. Essays on essential Miltonic topics.

Background

ABERCROMBIE, L.: *The Epic: The art and craft of letters*, Secker, London, 1914. Characteristics and history of epic poetry.

BOWRA, C.M.: *From Virgil to Milton*, Macmillan, London, 1945. Excellent in the evolution of epic.

CURRY, W.C.: *Milton's Ontology, Cosmogony and Physics*, University of Kentucky Press, Lexington, 1966.

NICOLSON, M.H.: *The Breaking of the Circle*, Oxford University Press, London, 1960. Excellent on the cosmological background of the seventeenth century.

The author of these notes

Richard James Beck OBE was educated at Jesus College, Oxford. His studies were interrupted by the war in which he served as a bomber pilot from 1940, being shot down in 1942 and spending three and a half years as a prisoner of war. He was a lecturer at the University of St Andrews (which awarded him a PHD in 1954) until becoming Professor of English at the University of Malta. His publications include an edition of Chaucer's *Preamble and Tale of the Wife of Bath* (Oliver and Boyd, Edinburgh, 1964); a critical introduction to Shakespeare's *Henry IV* (No. 24 in Arnold's *Studies in Literature*, London, 1965). He also published various articles in learned journals, principally on Chaucer and Milton. Professor Beck died in 1979.

The first 100 titles

CHINUA ACHEBE	*Arrow of God* *Things Fall Apart*
JANE AUSTEN	*Northanger Abbey* *Pride and Prejudice* *Sense and Sensibility*
ROBERT BOLT	*A Man For All Seasons*
CHARLOTTE BRONTË	*Jane Eyre*
EMILY BRONTË	*Wuthering Heights*
ALBERT CAMUS	*L'Etranger (The Outsider)*
GEOFFREY CHAUCER	*Prologue to the Canterbury Tales* *The Franklin's Tale* *The Knight's Tale* *The Nun's Priest's Tale* *The Pardoner's Tale*
SIR ARTHUR CONAN DOYLE	*The Hound of the Baskervilles*
JOSEPH CONRAD	*Nostromo*
DANIEL DEFOE	*Robinson Crusoe*
CHARLES DICKENS	*David Copperfield* *Great Expectations*
GEORGE ELIOT	*Adam Bede* *Silas Marner* *The Mill on the Floss*
T.S. ELIOT	*The Waste Land*
WILLIAM FAULKNER	*As I Lay Dying*
F. SCOTT FITZGERALD	*The Great Gatsby*
E.M. FORSTER	*A Passage to India*
ATHOL FUGARD	*Selected Plays*

MRS GASKELL	*North and South*
WILLIAM GOLDING	*Lord of the Flies*
OLIVER GOLDSMITH	*The Vicar of Wakefield*
THOMAS HARDY	*Jude the Obscure* *Tess of the D'Urbervilles* *The Mayor of Casterbridge* *The Return of the Native* *The Trumpet Major*
L.P. HARTLEY	*The Go-Between*
ERNEST HEMINGWAY	*For Whom the Bell Tolls* *The Old Man and the Sea*
ANTHONY HOPE	*The Prisoner of Zenda*
RICHARD HUGHES	*A High Wind in Jamaica*
THOMAS HUGHES	*Tom Brown's Schooldays*
HENRIK IBSEN	*A Doll's House*
HENRY JAMES	*The Turn of the Screw*
BEN JONSON	*The Alchemist* *Volpone*
D.H. LAWRENCE	*Sons and Lovers* *The Rainbow*
HARPER LEE	*To Kill a Mocking-Bird*
SOMERSET MAUGHAM	*Selected Short Stories*
HERMAN MELVILLE	*Billy Budd* *Moby Dick*
ARTHUR MILLER	*Death of a Salesman* *The Crucible*
JOHN MILTON	*Paradise Lost I & II*
SEAN O'CASEY	*Juno and the Paycock*
GEORGE ORWELL	*Animal Farm* *Nineteen Eighty-four*
JOHN OSBORNE	*Look Back in Anger*
HAROLD PINTER	*The Birthday Party*
J.D. SALINGER	*The Catcher in the Rye*

SIR WALTER SCOTT	*Ivanhoe*
	Quentin Durward
WILLIAM SHAKESPEARE	*A Midsummer Night's Dream*
	Antony and Cleopatra
	Coriolanus
	Cymbeline
	Hamlet
	Henry IV Part I
	Henry V
	Julius Caesar
	King Lear
	Macbeth
	Measure for Measure
	Othello
	Richard II
	Romeo and Juliet
	The Merchant of Venice
	The Tempest
	The Winter's Tale
	Troilus and Cressida
	Twelfth Night
GEORGE BERNARD SHAW	*Androcles and the Lion*
	Arms and the Man
	Caesar and Cleopatra
	Pygmalion
RICHARD BRINSLEY SHERIDAN	*The School for Scandal*
JOHN STEINBECK	*Of Mice and Men*
	The Grapes of Wrath
	The Pearl
ROBERT LOUIS STEVENSON	*Kidnapped*
	Treasure Island
JONATHAN SWIFT	*Gulliver's Travels*
W.M. THACKERAY	*Vanity Fair*
MARK TWAIN	*Huckleberry Finn*
	Tom Sawyer
VOLTAIRE	*Candide*
H.G. WELLS	*The History of Mr Polly*
	The Invisible Man
	The War of the Worlds
OSCAR WILDE	*The Importance of Being Earnest*